W9-BYL-356

WHAT DO I DO WHEN TEENAGERS ARE DEPRESSED AND CONTEMPLATE SUICIDE?

Dr. Steven Gerali

 ZONDERVAN®

ZONDERVAN.com/
AUTHORTRACKER
follow your favorite authors

 youth
specialties

YOUTH SPECIALTIES

What Do I Do When Teenagers Are Depressed and Contemplate Suicide?
Copyright 2009 by Steve Gerali

Youth Specialties resources, 1890 Cordell Ct. Ste. 105, El Cajon, CA 92020 are published by Zondervan, 5300 Patterson Ave. SE, Grand Rapids, MI 49530.

ISBN 978-0-310-29196-1

All Scripture quotations, unless otherwise indicated, are taken from the Holy Bible, *Today's New International Version*™. *TNIV*®. Copyright 2001, 2005 by Biblica, Inc.™ Used by permission of Zondervan. All rights reserved worldwide.

Any Internet addresses (websites, blogs, etc.) and telephone numbers printed in this book are offered as a resource. They are not intended in any way to be or imply an endorsement by Youth Specialties, nor does Youth Specialties vouch for the content of these sites and numbers for the life of this book.

All rights reserved. No part of this publication may be reproduced, stored in a retrieval system, or transmitted in any form or by any means — electronic, mechanical, photocopy, recording, or any other — except for brief quotations in printed reviews, without the prior permission of the publisher.

Cover design by Invisible Creature
Interior design by Brandi Etheredge Design

Printed in the United States of America

10 11 12 13 14 15 • 20 19 18 17 16 15 14 13 12 11 10 9 8 7 6 5 4 3 2

Contents

1.1 Definition and Scope
1.1A Depression
1.1B Physiology of Adolescent Depression
1.1C Myths about Teenage Depression
1.1D Common Symptoms and Warning Signs of Teenage Depression
1.1E Suicide

1.2 Forms of Depression
1.2A Dysthymia
1.2B Bipolar Disorder
1.2C Major Depressive Disorder
1.2D Seasonal Affective Disorder
1.2E Masked Depression
1.2F Situational Depression
1.2G Premenstrual Dysphoric Disorder

1.3 Suicide
1.3A Reasons Teenagers Contemplate Suicide
1.3B Myths about Teen Suicide
1.3C Signs and Symptoms
1.3D Suicide and Gay Teenagers
1.3E Suicide and Bullied Teenagers
1.3F Cluster Suicides

2.1 Theology That Informs Issues Related to Depression and Suicide
2.1A Theology That Informs Our Views of Depression
2.1B Theology of Suicide
2.1C Theology of Hope and Restoration
2.1D Theology of Healing (Medications)

What Do I Do When...
BOOK SERIES
|INTRODUCTION|
Read This First!

It's very important you read this Introduction. This series of books has grown out of years of listening to professional and volunteer youth workers wrestle through difficult ministry situations. I usually know what's coming when the conversation starts with, "What do I do when...?" Most of the time they're looking for remedial help, but many times the issues covered in this book series have no preventive measures available. Many of these issues aren't given serious thought until they evidence themselves in the fabric of ministry. Then youth workers, church staff, parents, and even teenagers scramble to get some kind of understanding, remedy, support, or theological perspective on the situation. This series is designed to help you.

Before we move too far ahead, you need to know a few things. First, just because you read these books and acquire some helping skills, that doesn't make you a professional counselor or caregiver. In many situations you'll need to help parents and teenagers network with professional mental health workers, medical professionals, or, in some cases, legal counsel. Oftentimes the quality of care regarding these issues lies in the rapid response of helping professionals. So if you don't get anything else out of this series, get this:

The best thing you can do as an effective helper is realize you're not a trained counselor and you must refer, refer, refer.

Second, often when youth workers are in the throes of an issue, they'll quickly access the Internet for help and information. Researching something online can be very time-consuming, and it can provide unreliable information. So this book series is designed to offer reliable information that's quickly accessible for anyone who's working with adolescents.

Third, each book follows a similar format designed to help you navigate the information more easily. But more importantly, it also provides a model to help you deal with the issue at hand. What Do I Do When... books are divided into the following four sections:

SECTION 1: UNDERSTANDING THE ISSUE, OR "PRESENTING PROBLEM"

Each book will start with an *epistemology* of the issue—in other words, the knowledge regarding its nature and scope. Many youth workers formulate their opinions, beliefs, and ideas using faulty information that's been passed through the grapevine—often without realizing the grapevine has root rot. Faulty information can change the trajectory of our actions in such a way it actually causes us to miss the mark. And many times our "misses" can be destructive to a kid who's already struggling with a painful issue.

We cannot expect to lead a teenager to the truth of Scripture if we start with a foundation that's built upon a lie or deception. We must be informed, seeking to understand the presenting problem as learners with a teachable spirit. In some cases these books may provide only the basics about an issue. But hopefully they'll be enough to create a solid foundation that gives direction for further research from reliable sources.

SECTION 2: UNDERSTANDING HOW YOUR THEOLOGY INTERSECTS THE ISSUE, OR PRESENTING PROBLEM

Each book will also cover at least one theological perspective that informs the situation. However, please note I plan to give theological insights from multiple perspectives, so you'll know the theological voices adolescents and their families hear. Some of these voices may not resonate with your particular view, but it's important you develop a gracious, loving, and understanding heart. Keep in mind you're dealing with desperate, hurting, and broken people who—in the midst of their pain and struggle—are seeking grace and hope, not someone with theological answers.

I realize there's a danger in writing like this. Whenever the playing field is leveled—in other words, when one's internalized theological framework is challenged or an opposing theological view is given—it can quickly become a fisticuffs arena to champion truth. I believe that truth brings freedom (John 8:32). But let's remember that the Pharisees believed they'd cornered the market on truth simply because they held to a rigid interpretation of the Scriptures, yet they failed to listen for God's voice in others—especially in the Messiah.

A dear friend of mine once confronted a group of students by asking, "Is your interpretation of Scripture always right?"

The students knew that if they replied affirmatively, then they'd set themselves up as the source of infallibility. So they replied, "No, nobody can be right all the time."

My friend then asked, "In what areas are you wrong?"

His wisdom during that loving confrontation helped those students see that unless they openly and graciously engaged the theological perspectives of others, they'd never know if their own perspectives were lacking. Our goal in helping kids through difficult issues is to usher Christ into their situations. Many times that may not be with answers but with presence, affection, support, and understanding.

I recall a situation in which my dear, sweet, Italian mother was hurting for a young couple who'd been caught in sexual sin (she and my dad had mentored this couple). The disciplinary actions of the church were harsh and shaming. So while the church acted in rightness, it failed to see other theological perspectives that informed this situation, such as a theology of reconciliation, grace, confession, and absolution. In my conversation with my mother, I heard her engage these things because she, too, entered into the process and pain of this young couple, and she refused to apply a static template of dealing with the issue in a "right way." Instead, she decided to deal with the issue first in a loving and good way.

It's important to remember that many times rightness is not goodness. God has called his people to be good (Matthew 5:16, Ephesians 2:10, 1 Timothy 6:17-19)—not always "right." That doesn't mean we ignore truth, nor does it mean we minimize the authority of Scripture. It just means we must be incredibly and painfully careful to err on the side of that which is loving and good. Wrestling through various theological viewpoints, even if we don't initially agree with them, will keep us in the tension of being loving and good.

SECTION 3: CONSIDERING WHAT ACTIONS WE CAN TAKE

When we understand an issue or problem, we must wrestle through the theological and consider appropriate action. That can mean anything from doing more research to aggressively seeking solutions. In this third section, I'll attempt to provide you with a framework for action, including practical examples, applications, and tips. This will only be a skeletal plan you'll need to own and tweak to fit the uniqueness of your situation. There is rarely one prescribed action for an issue—every situation is unique because of the people involved.

Throughout the years, I've watched youth workers attempt to use books about youth ministry as one uses an instruction manual for the assembly of a bicycle. They assume that if they put this screw into this hole, then this part will operate correctly. Likewise, they expect that applying a tip from a book will fix a student or situation. If only life were this easy!

Every example provided in this series of books grows out of my years of ministry and clinical experience, input from God's people, and proven results. But they're not foolproof solutions. God desires to be intimately involved in the lives of students and their families, as they trust in God through their difficult times. There is no fix-all formula—just faithfulness. So as you follow some of the directives or action steps in these books, remember you must prayerfully seek God in the resolution of the issues.

SECTION 4: ADDITIONAL RESOURCES

In this section I'll provide some reliable resources for further help. These Internet sites, books, and organizations can assist you in mobilizing help for teenagers and their families. Hopefully this will save you many hours of hunting, so you can better invest in your students and their families.

Where needed, I'll also give a brief comment or description for the source. For example, some sources will serve to explain a different theological perspective from mainstream. This will help you to be informed before you run out and buy the book or engage the Web site.

I trust this book series will assist you in the critical care of teenagers and their families. God has put you on the front lines of attending, shepherding, and training people who are very dear and valuable to his heart. The way you respond to each person who's involved in these critical issues may have eternal consequences. My prayer is that everyone who reads these books will be empowered in a new way to usher Jesus more deeply and practically into the lives of precious teenagers.

Understanding Depression and Suicide

| Section 1 |

1.1 DEFINITION AND SCOPE

The Raymond family started coming to our church last year. Christy Raymond was a junior, and her younger brother Justin was a freshman. The family had always lived in our community, and they (with a number of other families) started attending our church when their church merged with ours.

Both Christy and Justin got involved in our youth ministry. They had many friends there, went to the same school with a number of the students, and were involved in other activities in the community. They seemed to be well-networked.

The Raymond family was a very stable and loving family. They encouraged, disciplined, engaged, and were actively involved in the lives of their two teenage children. They encouraged them to follow their passions, develop their talents, and enjoy life. They had a very realistic outlook, cheering their children on to do their best but not putting pressure on them to overachieve.

Mrs. Raymond helped provide food and transportation when our youth ministry needed it. Mr. Raymond stepped in as often as he could and was extremely supportive of the youth ministry.

Together they opened their home to teens and the youth ministry and created very healthy boundaries for their own children as well as the others who frequented their home.

Christy was a vivacious, energetic, and relationally engaging young woman. She loved Jesus, and she planned to live life to its fullest. She was active in everything from sports to social concerns. You only had to be around her for a few minutes before you realized this girl was going to become a great woman. Christy got involved in a small group and became a motivating force for the cohesiveness of the group and the spiritual growth of the other girls in her group. Her small-group leader loved having Christy in the group.

Justin seemed to be the mirror opposite of his sister and his family. He was irritable. It seemed like he hated everyone. He was disrespectful, pessimistic, and often seemed to be in another world. His small-group leader, Chuck, went out of his way to connect with Justin, but every conversation was an uphill battle.

The only thing that seemed to interest Justin was sports. He spent hours in front of the TV watching game after game. Justin was a great athlete, too, so his dad encouraged him to get involved in sports at school, hoping that would change Justin's negative outlook on life. Justin started every sport well. His coaches would invest a lot of time in him (though some didn't tolerate his negativity) and were amazed at his natural ability. But a few weeks into each practice season, Justin would quit. But he wouldn't tell his parents he quit and pretended to be at practice.

After youth group one night Chuck pulled me aside. "Justin is killing my small group. He's so negative, and I just can't seem to connect with him. I feel like I'm giving him three times more energy and attention than any other guy in my group. I really think something is wrong. What should I do?"

Justin had a dysthymic disorder—in other words, he was chronically depressed. His parents thought this was just a stage of teenage angst—that is, until Justin started to verbalize and write about his morbid ideations of death. They immediately got help for their son.

Maybe you're in the same place as Chuck—you're trying to help a difficult teenager, but you're coming to the end of your rope. Maybe you have a teenager like Justin in your group.

Adolescent depression is complex and difficult to diagnose. It can be draining for parents and youth workers. It can be deadly for teens who experience constant emotional pain, hopelessness, and sadness. This despair can move teens to believe the only way out is death. The good news is that adolescent depression can be treated, and depressed teens can go on to live happier, productive lives.

This book will help you understand adolescent depression and its various forms as well as give you some theological points of reference that can inform your interactions with depressed teens and their families. My hope is to give you some effective steps when faced with the question, "What do I do when teenagers are depressed and contemplate suicide?"

1.1A DEPRESSION

Depression is probably one of the most common and pervasive struggles teenagers deal with over the course of their adolescence. Yet most youth workers don't know much about adolescent depression or how to help a teen hurting in this way. Many people, including parents and youth workers, dismiss it as a part of the hormonal-emotive roller coaster brought on by this developmental stage. Depression is an "affect" disorder, and while that can sound scary, it should be noted all people experience depression in some form during the course of their lives.

In its mildest form, depression is as common as an ordinary cold. Medical health professionals estimate that one in eight American teenagers suffer from some form of depression[1]; that's more than 3.5 million teens. This is only an estimate based on diagnosed cases of depression.

It's likely that many more teens experience some form of depression than the statistics reveal. Estimates may be low because, as noted previously, adolescent depression is often chalked up to normal teenage emotional immaturity. It can also go unreported because teenagers may not have the capacity to label their feelings. When asked, they may replay that they don't know what they feel, or that they feel...bad. Depression or any form of sadness is often retranslated into some form of angst.

Guys, in particular, often lack the emotive perception that girls typically have already developed. A girl also possesses the verbal skills a teenage guy often lacks. The combination makes it easier for a teenage girl to identify and verbalize feelings. In addition, a teenage guy may not report feeling sad or depressed because sadness is perceived as emotional weakness. Guys are often raised to embrace masculine bravado that requires them to always be in control of feelings.

What makes it more challenging is that the word *depression* has so many different meanings in our society. Teens use it as a description for disappointment ("I was so depressed when they cancelled the field trip") or for negative experiences ("Today was a depressing day") or as an act of empathy ("That's such depressing news").

Because girls are more in touch with their emotions than guys, it's often believed that teenage girls suffer from depression more than teenage guys. In truth, depression affects all teens regardless of gender, ethnicity, race, or socioeconomic status. Depressed teens are also at higher risk for substance abuse, struggles at school and work, relational problems, conflict and antisocial behaviors, risky sexual behaviors, and suicide.

Many of the teenagers in our ministries struggle with depression. But again, the good news is that depression can be successfully treated. Therefore, youth workers should know the facts, signs, and symptoms of adolescent depression so they can refer teens and their families to counselors or mental health professionals.

1.1B PHYSIOLOGY OF ADOLESCENT DEPRESSION

Brain chemicals, called neurotransmitters, are the physiological cause of depression. The limbic system of the brain is responsible for the control of emotion, stress responses (physiological and emotional), and physical and sexual urges and drives. The limbic system produces neurotransmitters, specifically serotonin, norepinephrine, and dopamine, all of which help to regulate mood and emotion. These chemicals are responsible for transferring information in the form of electrical impulses to and from the hundred billion-plus neurons, or nerve cells, throughout the brain. Whenever we process anything mentally, these neurons are triggered as electrical impulses travel across them in about 1/15,000[th] of a second. This allows our brains to quickly react to stimuli and yield thought and emotion. The electrical impulse is then picked up by the dendrite (one of the spindly arms of the neuron), travels through the body of the neuron, and then down the axon where it's converted to a chemical or neurotransmitter. The neurotransmitter then carries the impulse across the synapses (gaps between the neurons) to the receptors in the dendrite of another neuron where it becomes electrical again. The dendrite receptors are like locks that receive only certain types of neurotransmitter keys. If the wrong key goes to a lock, an imbalance can occur and the receptor will reject the neurotransmitter. Then it will either lie dormant in the synapses where it's broken down by other chemicals, or it will be sent back to the neuron that released it (aka the reuptake process).

The production of certain neurotransmitters and this chemical imbalance can cause certain mood swings and depression. These negative results are difficult to control because they're due to reflexive cause and effect: Thought and behavior can affect this brain chemistry, and brain chemistry can affect thought and behavior. This vicious cycle can spiral out of control and lead the individual into a major depression. This is why antidepressants, or reuptake inhibitors, as well as psychotherapy, are essential to effectively treat major depression.

In addition, adults and teens process neurological activity quite differently. Throughout the normal day in the lives of adults, we experience information and stimuli through our senses. This information is translated into electrical current in the brain, producing thought and behavior and affecting mood. These thoughts and behaviors also affect emotion, creating a cycle of process. For example, someone may inform you your cat was run over by a car. You immediately respond with joy because you hated that cat, or you may feel sad but not devastated because it was just a cat, or you may feel grief because the cat was a part of your family. The way you respond is largely due to the types and uninhibited flow of the neurotransmitters in your brain and the thought processes you go through. If you process that news lightly, for example, it will yield a sad but non depressive emotion; moments later you can respond to another situation with joy or many other emotions.

For a teenager, however, this emotive ebb and flow has a wider range and more volatile swing. This is due to the fact that teenagers are not as cognitively mature—they don't process information and emotions as quickly because they don't have the abstract reasoning skills or life experiences of an adult. A teenager may hear that the cat was killed, and this may cause great distress even if the cat was insignificant to the teen. That teen's brain may trigger an avalanching effect that causes her to have a greater range of emotion.

So while adults can have a series of negative and positive emotions in one day, the number of negative emotions may outweigh the positive (or vice-versa), a negatively emotional day doesn't make an adult emotionally dysfunctional. For teenagers the emotive swing may be greater and last much longer. It may even last for a few days. That, however, may not mean teenagers are experiencing depression.

Parents and youth workers need to understand that teen emotions are in an exaggerated state. But again, this makes depression very difficult to diagnose as it's hard to distinguish from normal aspects of a teen's developmental stage.

Factors that can affect brain chemistry also include heredity, life stressors, negative thought patterns, certain illnesses, medications, alcohol and drug abuse, lack of sunlight, and environmental and hormonal changes. As you're aware, teenagers are hormone factories. The hypothalamus in the brain is the bridge between the limbic system and the endocrine system. The hypothalamus directly activates the pituitary gland, which links a hypothalamic-pituitary-gonadal (HPG) axis, all initiating and maintaining the production of many hormones. In teenagers, the hormones known as gonadotropins (estrogen, progesterone, and testosterone) begin the process of puberty and sexual maturation. These hormones, with many others, are released into the bloodstream. The hormones that don't control sexual development and drive help the body regulate reaction to stress. The endocrine system constantly monitors production of these hormones.

If any hormone level gets too high, the producing gland is signaled to shut down by the endocrine system. This can be likened to a circuit breaker. However, this signaling process can often fail when a person is in a depressed state. This hormonal irregularity can factor into depression and physical stress reactions such as sleep and appetite. Because the hypothalamus links the limbic and endocrine systems, it uses neurotransmitters in the role of hormonal production as it regulates the pituitary gland and other glands of the endocrine system. If the neurotransmitters become imbalanced it may also affect hormones. Teenagers with an overload of hormones aren't necessarily in a state of depression; extreme hormonal production may affect adolescents' exaggerated mood swings, but it won't keep them locked in a depressive state. Still, adolescent depression may be affected when certain hormones are not regulated (albeit in excess) along with other hormones.

This may seem like a lot of scientific information to digest. But it's important for parents and youth workers to understand the physiological factors in adolescent depression so they may also understand the role antidepressant medications can play in helping regulate chemical imbalances that lead to teen depression.

For the record, antidepressants often carry a negative stigma, viewed as addictive medications that have damaging effects. This is not true. In fact, for some people these medications provide the same service in regulating depression as insulin does in regulating diabetes. Both diseases are the result of chemical deficiencies in the body. If the body is incapable of producing needed chemicals, then they must be introduced through medication. In the case of antidepressants, affected people may not need to be on them all their lives. For example, if an antidepressant jumpstarts the production and balance of neurotransmitters, then the medication may be decreased and then ceased all together. If antidepressants are decreased and the depressive state still exists, that indicates the brain isn't producing the needed neurotransmitters.

I've talked to many parents who have a skewed perception of antidepressants. They refuse to put their teens on medications for fear they'll become mind-altered. I often suggest they see psychiatrists who can regulate doses properly. But just like the negative perception of antidepressants, the idea of taking your teenager to a psychiatrist carries equal baggage. Many parents believe psychiatrists are only for people who are crazy or have intense mental issues, so they take their sons or daughters to the family physician or pediatrician instead. While pediatricians are licensed to administer antidepressants, most often they're not trained or qualified to make the correct diagnoses or regulate the appropriate medications and doses necessary for teenagers' mental health. This is why so many teens who take antidepressants prescribed by their family physicians appear lethargic and sedated. Seeing a qualified doctor who specializes in adolescent psychiatry is the better course of action. Counseling, balanced in conjunction with antidepressants, can combat the physiological factors and distorted thought patterns depression causes.

1.1C MYTHS ABOUT TEENAGE DEPRESSION

It's just a part of adolescence. This myth is built on the premise teens are always on an emotional roller coaster, so either they can't get depressed or they're always depressed. Without question, teens are often moody, so depression can be mistaken as part of that moodiness. But that same emotional swing brought about by the developmental process can also hide the severity of a teen's depression. Adolescent depression is a serious issue and should not be looked upon as a stage teens will grow out of.

It's a part of culturally induced angst. In other words, teens are conditioned by culture to be angry, apathetic, and depressed, and they're just playing out the expected roles and scripts. Prior to the 1950s, the mental health community believed that children and youth could not experience the breadth of emotion adults experience. These conclusions were rooted in psychoanalytic views that the teenager's ego (identity) isn't developed and therefore is unable to formulate more complex emotions. As a result, depression in teens was viewed as a mimicked or learned behavior. To the contrary, depression is not among the repertoire of cultural behaviors teens attempt to emulate. Depression in teenagers is a real and critical issue that shouldn't be passed off lightly. Teenagers are very capable of feeling a full range of emotions, including the depths of depression.

It's not as bad as it seems because teens exaggerate. Exaggeration may indeed be part of the extreme behaviors that often come with adolescence. There are attention-seeking teens and others who are histrionic. But this myth is dangerous because it minimizes the severity of adolescent depression. Many parents who've experienced the suicide of their children often confess they didn't think their depression was as bad as their teenagers were making it out to be. Minimizing a teenager's, or for that matter anyone's, pain is a foolish practice. Comments such as, "It's really not that bad" or, "Things will be better tomorrow" are dismissive of the pain and sorrow a teen feels—and erode the teen's hope and confidence. This can plunge a teen deeper into depression. Consequently, depression must be treated seriously, even if the teenager is truly faking it.

Teenagers will tell you if they're depressed. Many times after a teen's suicide, friends and parents are shocked because they didn't see it coming. Teenagers can experience very severe depression without ever communicating what they're feeling. They may not have the cognitive skills to wrap language around the complexity of negative feelings they are experiencing. In addition, teenage guys don't typically develop emotional vocabulary and intuitiveness as quickly or as well as teenage girls. A depressed teenage guy therefore becomes a greater risk of oversight by someone who holds to this myth. Teenagers may not be able to tell you they're depressed—this is why it's so vital that youth workers and parents recognize the warning signs of adolescent depression.

It's a spiritual deficiency in the teenager. Some who hold to this myth believe that depression is rooted in a lack of faith, sin, or a broken relationship with God. Some may also believe that illness and disease are the consequences of a weak spiritual condition. Later in this book we'll examine the theology that informs our views on depression. For now, understand that this myth can be the sorce of discouragement and deeper depression to a teen who believes that he or she is spiritually deficient, works hard to overcome it, and then still remains caught in the grip of depression.

Depressed teens tend to be loners. At the core of this myth is the belief that teens who have friends don't get depressed—only the loners get depressed! There are no statistics that validate the notion that heavily networked teens (or adults) experience less depression than those with few or no friends. But the fact is, teenagers who are well-networked can experience severe depression. At the same time, withdrawal and isolation can be a symptom of depression, but even then some teens can stay connected to friends and be hiding a lot of emotional pain.

Tough love can make a teenager snap out of depression. Depression can be taxing on everyone. Many parents and youth workers lose their patience with depressed teens. They believe that an effective tactic is to level sanctions to make them "will away" their depression. The premise that drives this myth is that depression is an act of volition—teenagers are depressed because they choose to be, and therefore they can choose *not* to be depressed. Tough love is then used with the intention of breaking the will of the teenager, jarring him out of the gloomy state. We'll unpack this faulty thinking more when we examine some tips to help families who have depressed teens. For now, we must understand that depressed teens do not choose their depression, nor can they just will it away. Sanctions against depressed teens can only push them into deeper depression by validating feelings of abnormality, lack of love, and diminished value. A tough love approach can also be the final variable that pushes the teen toward suicide.

Antidepressants are harmful to teenagers. A quick search on the Internet unearths all sorts of false statements that raise fears about antidepressants. One recent rumor centered on a study that identified suicidal thoughts as a side effect of antidepressant use among teens and children. This escalated fear in many parents who believed that antidepressants weren't safe for teenagers. While there are risks and side effects for any medication, it doesn't mean everyone will experience those effects. Untreated depression puts teens at the greatest risk of suicide.

1.1D COMMON SYMPTOMS AND WARNING SIGNS OF TEENAGE DEPRESSION

There are a number of symptoms parents and youth workers should be on the alert for, which are indicative of any type of depression. The degree to which these symptoms are present could indicate the extent to which a teen is depressed.

Emotional Disposition. Depressed teens often have pervasive feelings of sadness, despair, hopelessness, guilt, shame, worthlessness, anger, or fear, and also feel hurt, unloved, and irritable.

Verbal Cues. Written and orally expressed, verbal cues are often the best clues for adults into the despair depressed teens are experiencing. Verbal cues also are good indicators of teens' thought patterns and self-perception.

- "Nobody likes me."
- "Something bad is going to happen."
- "I'm never going to be happy again."
- "Life sucks—I'm such a loser."
- "I just don't want to get out of bed anymore."

Behavioral Cues. Isolating and withdrawing from friends and family; constantly tearing up or crying; easily set off, bothered, or angered; moping and spending hours in front of the TV; failing to complete schoolwork or other tasks of responsibility; and having difficulty remembering things; are some of the behaviors of a depressed teen.

Changes in Sleep Patterns. This can present in two ways, either sleeping more (longer periods of time to more frequently throughout the day) or sleeping less (shorter periods of time marked by insomnia or frequently waking up at night). The latter tends to be more prominent with depressed teens. They may also show signs of constant fatigue and lethargy, lacking energy and motivation. They may comment about having a heavy feeling about them.

Changes in Eating Patterns. This can swing either direction. Depressed teens may experience loss of appetite and not eat at all. This could evidence itself in rapid weight loss. On the other hand they may binge eat and begin to put on weight. Other changes in eating patterns could include eating more junk foods, nausea at the smell or thought of food, or eating at atypical times.

Shifts in Appearance. One common way depression is seen is when teens no longer seem to care about grooming and hygiene. Depressed teens who were once meticulous about their appearance won't shower, comb their hair, use deodorant, or brush their teeth. They may want to stay in the same clothes for days, even sleeping in them. Depression may also evidence itself by the appearance of teens' bedrooms. They may post morbid posters, display depressing song lyrics and poems, or desire to paint their walls black. They may also wear dark clothing, makeup (or lack of it), and accessories. While Goth is a style that some perfectly healthy, nondepressed teens adopt, it can become a magnet for depressed teens. They may show a sudden interest in piercing, branding, and tattooing as well. While these may be acceptable fashion statements, one must be aware that depressed teens often gravitate toward lingering physical pain to take their minds off emotional pain.

Risky Behaviors. Depressed teens often look for ways of escape—everything from an adrenaline rush (e.g., driving fast, unprotected sexual activity, or shoplifting or other illegal activities) to take their minds off the depression to inflicting some form of physical pain (e.g., cutting, burning, pulling out hair, etc.) to overpower the depression to anesthetizing the pain of depression (e.g., experimenting with, using, and abusing alcohol and other drugs.)

Anhedonia. The inability to gain any kind of pleasure from anything. Depressed teens may not find joy in the things they enjoyed in the past and appear passionless. Even things like food, music, video games, and friends are no longer interesting or satisfying. This tends to be more identifiable in depressed teenage guys than girls. The loss of pleasure may also have a backlash effect. As anhedonia sets in, teens may binge in pleasurable activities to keep pleasure alive and satiate depression. For example a teen may stay up all night playing video games, or listen to the same song over and over, or masturbate much more than usual.

Suicide. Depression often precedes suicide. The more severe the depression, the closer the teen may come to committing suicide. Depressed teens may show signs of suicide ideation, strategy, and even attempts.

1.1E SUICIDE

Suicide is a serious public health problem among the global adolescent population. The World Health Organization (WHO) notes that suicide among adolescents (ages 15 to19) is increasing in 90 of the 130 countries that are members.[2] Worldwide, suicide is ranked as the fourth-leading cause of death for teenage males and third for female teens. In many member countries suicide is the leading cause of death among adolescents.[3]

These statistics may be greatly under reported because many of the countries in the organization have cultural and religious stigmas associated with suicide. This is such a major concern that the World Medical Association (WMA) adopted a policy statement on Adolescent Suicide at the 1991 World Medical Assembly in Malta and then revised it through the WMA General Assembly in South Africa in 2006. This policy outlines guidelines requiring medical professionals to be made aware, trained, and to provide preventive measures for adolescents at risk of suicide.[4]

According to the U.S. Centers for Disease Control (CDC), between 2000 and 2006, suicide was the third leading cause of death among all pre-adolescents and adolescents (ages 10 to 24) in the United States.[5] Homicide was the second-leading cause and accidental death was first. It's difficult to tell how many of those accidental deaths were, in fact, suicides. Many automobile crashes, drug overdoses, drownings, and falls could be suicides but are reported as accidental deaths. Given that speculation, suicide may be the second-leading cause of death among adolescents in the United States. In the same report, suicide was ranked as the second-leading cause of death among Asian American and white adolescents (ages 15 to 24) and American Indian adolescents (ages 10 to 24).

The CDC also identified the three leading methods of adolescent suicide: Use of firearms, suffocation, and poisoning—they make up 50.9 percent, 33.4 percent, and 8.2 percent— of all U.S. adolescent deaths. Other methods used by adolescents were deliberate fatal falls, self-inflicted wounds such as cutting and piercing, drowning, and setting oneself on fire. While these methods were the same ones younger adolescents (ages 10 to 14) used, suicide by suffocation was highest among the younger age group at 62.3 percent and suicide with a firearm at 30.6 percent.[6]

The U.S. Department of Health and Human Services, Office of the Surgeon General, reported that between 1952 and 1996 the suicide rate among adolescents and young adults has tripled. It was also noted that between 1980 and 1996 the rate of suicide among adolescents (ages 15 to 19) increased by 14 percent and among younger adolescents (ages 10 to 14) by 100 percent. For African American males (ages 15 to 19), the rate increased 105 percent, although white males of the same age are at greatest risk of suicide.[7] In 2007 the CDC cited that 14.5 percent of high school students claimed they had seriously contemplated suicide within the year prior to the survey, and 6.9 percent of those surveyed attempted suicide at least once during that year.[8] The CDC also noted there are about 25 suicide attempts among teens for every one completed suicide. Teenage suicide is and should be a critical concern among youth workers.

1.2 FORMS OF DEPRESSION

1.2A DYSTHYMIA

A mild, chronic form of depression, the word *dysthymia* means an ill state of mind. It's a low-grade depression where teens usually feel gloomy, heavy, unhappy, or irritable most of the day. Teens with dysthymic conditions describe their moods as "constantly feeling down" or "like a dark cloud follows them around."

Like Justin in the opening story, dysthymic teens may be able to function normally but also seem negative, disengaged, or pessimistic. They rarely feel joy or happiness and find little pleasure in anything. They usually experience the symptoms described previously but in a less severe or lower grade than in a major depression. Dysthymic depression is chronic, meaning that it occurs more days than it doesn't, can last longer than a year, and can continue for many years. In teens the condition is diagnosed if the depression has lasted longer than a year and presents with two or more of the symptoms above. Normally a teen with dysthymia can also experience mental health issue such as attention deficit disorder, a learning disorder, an eating disorder, conduct disorder, and so on. This combination—often referred to as double depression—is dangerous. When double depression occurs in teens, the normal lows they feel spiral out of control to greater depths. Double depression also is often marked by greater levels of hopelessness as well as intense suicide ideation.

1.2B BIPOLAR DISORDER

Bipolar disorder is a cyclical depression in which a teen fluctuates between manic (high) episodes and depressive (low) episodes—which is why it's also referred to as manic-depressive disorder. The highs and lows are two poles on either end of the emotional continuum, thus "bipolar."

Diagnosing bipolar disorder in teens is a very difficult process since adolescence is characterized by extreme emotional highs and lows, but the highs and lows tend to hit extreme severity in bipolar teens. In addition, bipolar disorder may also be misdiagnosed as schizophrenia, attention deficit disorder, conduct disorder, or major depressive disorder. Therefore diagnosing bipolar disorder involves long observation and charting of behaviors.

Adults with bipolar disorder tend to experience manic and depressive episodes in patterns usually lasting for weeks to months. Each episode can be followed by a period where they experience "normal," meaning they have a break between episodes where they function well or close to well. Teens, however, tend to experience manic and depressive episodes with greater irregularity, often in the course of the same day. They may also not have any break between the episodes, giving them a "Jekyll and Hyde" effect. There are also variations during which either the manic or depressive episodes are more prominent. Some believe that the manic episodes of this disorder are marked by happier times and tend to be the better side of the disorder, but this isn't true. Many times the manic episodes can be just as dangerous and concerning as the severe depression.

Symptoms of manic episodes:

Wide-ranging emotions: From giddy, agitated, irritable, obnoxious, and jittery to aggressive, angry, enraged, spiteful, and resentful.

Incessant talking: Teens may talk nonstop, sometimes without reason or awareness of context and without allowing anyone to interrupt them. They may change subjects without provocation as things pop into their minds. They also may fail to read social cues indicating that people around them are annoyed, aren't listening, or are disinterested.

Increased energy: They may not sleep for days because they run on high energy. This can also cause them to do bizarre things, especially while everyone else is sleeping (e.g., play loud music and dance in the backyard at 3 a.m.; paint the bedroom, car, and anything else desired; tear apart the kitchen and prepare a lot of food.) Sometimes this can play itself out in more positive ways (e.g., a teen with artistic skills may paint for days without stopping—but if she's disturbed, she may also go into a fit of rage).

Unrealistic self-perceptions: They often overestimate who they are, what they can accomplish, and what their limitations are. This behavior can range from grandiose talk to attempting feats of strength, skill, and competence beyond their abilities. This high can often resemble a drug high where bipolar teens believe they have superpowers. This may also be played out with attention-seeking behaviors, including being loud and obnoxious.

Engagement in high-risk, reckless activities: Fighting, vandalism, arson, drug and alcohol use and binging, excessive spending (sometimes taking parents' credit cards or forging checks), disturbing the peace, hypersexuality (including deviant sexual experimentation and promiscuity), reckless driving, and so on. These behaviors are often accompanied by a lack of judgment, rash and rapid decision making, and defiance of authority.

Other symptoms: Psychosis, or the inability to discern reality from fantasy (e.g., they may believe they're living in a video game); delusions (they may tell people they're personal friends with some teen idol or rock star, fabricating elaborate stories about their relationship); hallucinations (they may believe the patterns on their clothing are changing); and personality changes (shy, reserved teens may become extroverted or overtly sexual).

Symptoms of depressive episodes:

All the depressive symptoms listed previously. The difference with bipolar depression is there's a "crash" effect—the person is plummeted into the dark of sadness and anxiety. Suicide ideation and suicide attempts may be more exaggerated in the depressive episodes of bipolar teens as well.

Bipolar disorder can be treated through medication that works to reduce the number and intensity of the manic episodes and regulate the severity of the depressive episodes. Many times these medications are needed for long periods of time.

In addition, bipolar teens may need therapy for long periods of time. : It's important that these teens see mental-health clinicians who specialize in both adolescence and bipolar depression. Teens with bipolar depression often feel abnormal because of their emotional roller coaster swings that cause them to say and do things they would normally not say or do.. Sometimes they may also face criminal charges or may have violated their (and their families') morality. They may suffer guilt, shame, and devastation. Therapy helps to build their esteem and understanding of the complex issues that come with this type of depressive disorder. Important note: If bipolar depression isn't treated, the depressive episodes can become more severe in adulthood or can turn into a more severe major depression. NOTE: If bipolar depression isn't treated, the depressive episodes can become more severe in adulthood or can turn into more severe major depressions.

Also, teens may experience a variation of bipolar disorder known as a cyclothymic disorder—a milder form of bipolar disorder in which manic and depressive episodes aren't as frequent or severe. This is much more difficult to diagnose because the severity of bipolar disorders tend to be the diagnostic giveaways.

1.2C MAJOR DEPRESSIVE DISORDER

Major depressive disorder (or clinical depression) is a severe depression marked by pervasive sadness, despair, and hopelessness. It's more than a bad day, feeling unhappy, down, irritable, or moody for most of the day. This type of depression starts out with teens feeling sad, then it spirals down deeper and deeper until they feel hopeless. The depression becomes categorized as a major depression when it lasts longer than two weeks and five or more symptoms listed below are present that were otherwise not part of their lives.

For example, if a teen always had trouble sleeping, then that symptom wouldn't be a factor in determining the severity of the depression. In addition, the depression can be labeled "severe" or a "major depression" when it affects the teen's normal living patterns such as home life, school, social life, and work. A single episode of this depression can last one or two months to about nine months or more without the teen feeling any elevation in mood. Some teens can experience more than a single episode of major depression. A recurring major depression is defined by bouts of depression that last two weeks or longer followed by "normal" for a duration of time. This pattern then repeats itself. This is similar to bipolar disorder, only there are no manic episodes. Recurring major depression is marked by cycles of depression and can be very defeating to teens and their families.

The more common symptoms that mark major depression in teens are:

- Sadness, hopelessness, and despair.
- Lack of concentration marked by inability to track conversations or engage in life situations.

- Anhedonia (decreased interest in life activities or loss of pleasure from things that once brought pleasure).

- **Decreased appetite.** Teens may go for days without eating.

- **Increased sleep.** Normally a teenager needs about eight or nine hours of sleep per night; teens with major depression may sleep 12 or more hours in the course of a day. They also may wake up tired in the morning, sleep during the day or after school, and possibly fall asleep again sometime in the mid-evening.

- Fatigue and loss of energy, evidenced by teens verbalizing that their arms or legs feel heavy or having no energy or desire to keep proper hygiene or dress.

- Hypersensitivity including being fragile to criticism, negative comments, ordisapproval from others.

- Complaints of headaches, stomach aches, back pain, dizziness, or nausea.

- Isolation and withdrawal from friends and family as well as other relationship complications (such as believing that their friends are being disloyal, thinking their friends don't like them, fearing a romantic breakup, etc).

- Attempts at self-harm; most commonly cutting and binge drinking, but also branding, self-tattooing, and self-piercing.

- Suicide ideation, threats, plans, and attempts.

1.2D SEASONAL AFFECTIVE DISORDER

Teenagers with seasonal affective disorder (SAD) experience depression during season shifts (e.g., from summer to fall and then fall into winter). SAD is a cyclic disorder, meaning the depression recurs every year about the same time. SAD usually affects late adolescents (ages 18 to 22) and is more common in girls than guys. The younger the teenager, the less common SAD is. It's very uncommon to find a junior higher with this type of depression. This type of depression can range from mild dysthymic moods or feeling "down" to major depression where teens contemplate suicide. Many times the depression becomes more severe as the season progresses. Sometimes SAD is referred to as "winter depression," and it makes holidays difficult for many families. The lack of sunlight and change in climate when the autumn and winter seasons hit tend to affect mood. Therefore teenagers who live where the winters become pronounced and the days become much shorter (as with the northeast and north midwestern states) or in areas with long, pronounced rainy seasons (e.g., the Pacific Northwest) are more susceptible to SAD.

There's no conclusive evidence that pinpoints the cause of SAD, but factors that play into this disorder are:

- Some research shows that the lack of sunlight during a seasonal change can affect the body's natural clock or cycles (i.e., circadian rhythms). Circadian rhythms regulate the waking and sleeping balance of the body. In the normal course of the day an individual's body produces a hormone called melatonin. At mid-evening, when the sun begins to go down, the body begins to produce higher levels of melatonin. These levels continue to rise as it gets darker and cause the body to wind down, become sleepy, and keep the body in a sleepy state through the evening. Sunlight (or the lack thereof) affects melatonin production. In the winter months melatonin levels increase, and this higher level of melatonin in teenagers can make them more lethargic and fatigued. It may also cause shifts in sleep patterns, where teens find they sleep for shorter periods of time and more shallowly and frequently throughout the day. But while melatonin regulates sleep, it only plays a part in the circadian balance, so it's difficult to tell if it creates the imbalance that causes seasonal affective disorder.

- **Lack of sunlight can also cause a decrease in the serotonin levels in the brain.** As we discussed earlier, serotonin is a neurotransmitter that helps regulate mood. Lack of sunlight resulting in overcast, wintry days and longer nights can cause serotonin imbalances that are pronounced over the colder months, resulting in a seasonal depression.
- **There is some evidence of a genetic link to SAD.** Family histories show the presence of SAD along blood lines.

Like the other forms of depression, seasonal affective disorder is marked by many symptoms:

Pervasive sense of sadness. This can start out as a melancholy feeling, then progress into a deeper, pervasive sadness that immobilizes teens. Some believe it's brought on by the stress of the holidays and the accentuated family dysfunctions that often surround the holidays. Sometimes the depression continues beyond the holidays and becomes worse in late January and February.

Irritability and the inability to find pleasure in things that were previously pleasurable (e.g., being with friends, going to movies, listening to music, exercising talents, and so on).

Feelings of worthlessness, fear, hopelessness, sadness, unidentifiable guilt, and not being loved.

Changes in eating patterns. This shift is usually evidenced in overeating and eating unhealthy foods. Teens often crave carbohydrates; sweets and starchy foods become the staple. This often causes teens to put on weight.

Changes in sleep patterns. We've already discussed this, but take note that when teens are awake, they may seem more lethargic and apathetic. This constant fatigue can be misdiagnosed as chronic fatigue syndrome because of how long it can last.

Lack of concentration and diminished ability to reason. Everyday decisions can become marked by indecisiveness and stress. As a result, teens' grades may fall as homework isn't completed.

Dread and anxiety over holidays. The teen may experience the stress that accompanies holidays. This can give way to ideations of inadequacy, thoughts of relational conflicts and a hyper-sensitivity to family dynamics. Often the teen will seem to be more "fragile".

Many of these symptoms are the same as other forms of depression, which makes it difficult to distinguish SAD from other depressions. The criteria that distinguish SAD are two repeatable patterns:

1. The depression must occur at the same time each year over a minimum of two years.
2. The duration of the depression can't last longer than the duration of the season.

There are many ways seasonal affective disorder can be treated. Usually treatment begins with prescribed antidepressants—but while this may help regulate serotonin levels, it may not correct the depression. Melatonin dietary supplements can also be used to help balance the sleep cycle. The best treatment is known as light therapy, or phototherapy, in which a light box emits brighter and more focused light upon the teen, who sits nearby. Exposure to this light balances the body's natural production of melatonin and regulates the circadian cycles. The light box usually is made with fluorescent bulbs and is about 30 percent brighter than the soft light of a lamp. For treatment the teen can have the light box on while doing homework or any other activity for a period of 30 minutes to two hours depending on doctor's orders. But for best results it's recommended for mornings when the teen wakes up. Some of the side effects of phototherapy include headaches and eye strain.

1.2E MASKED DEPRESSION

Sometimes this type of depression is called atypical depression, and you can probably figure out what masked depression is from its label—it's difficult to detect or diagnose because the classic depression symptoms are overshadowed or "masked" by other symptoms or behaviors. Most of the time masked depression is identified by another problem (e.g., anxiety, stress, eating disorders, behavioral issues, being bullied or abused, substance abuse, physical ailments, learning disorders, etc.). These symptoms may take the spotlight and prevent the depression from ever being diagnosed. There are three additional common ways teenagers experience masked depression:

They may be irritable, sad, and moping the majority of the time. They may have difficulty sleeping and eating, feel worthless and unloved, show all the signs of depression to their parents, but...as soon as they're in face-to-face encounters with their friends, they perk up, smile, and engage them. This is a masked depression. Teens learn to live into personas they try not to compromise in any way. While they smile on the outside, their sadness eats away at them. One of the big symptoms they cannot hide, however, is lack of concentration. Their minds continue to dwell in the shadow of misery. It may appear to their friends that they're daydreaming, and adults may ask if they're okay, and their response will be (you know it), "I'm fine!"

Anger and aggression also mask depression. This form of masked depression is more common for teenage guys than girls, as most guys are always on "bravado alert." Their identities as (emerging) men mandate they be in control of their circumstances and emotions. They're also typically conditioned to not appear weak, show any signs of being sissies, and never cry. Therefore the sadness of depression violates everything they know to be masculine. This complicates the depression and yields a response or emotion that is acceptably masculine—rage. A teenage guy with masked depression may never cry, but he may get into frequent altercations, fly off the handle easily, or become verbally abusive. Parents comment that their sons "suddenly" have so much rage in them, and they try to control it through punishment, involvement in aggressive sports, or even sending them to military schools—only to find out that anger isn't the issue. A good adolescent therapist will begin by working through identity issues while dealing with the depression.

A third way depression is masked is through profound apathy and anhedonia. Both genders evidence apathy (or lack of passion and concern). Apathy that is masking depression is "profound" because it plays out in a disregard for others' trauma and tragedy as well as one's own trauma and tragedy. The difference in these teenagers from others who exhibit apathy and anhedonia along with depressive symptoms is that teens with this masked depression don't show the depressive symptoms and rarely withdraw or are isolated. They go through all the routines of the day appearing emotionally, morally, and socially flatlined. Because of the disregard for themselves, they take dangerous risks.

Both teenage girls and guys experience this masking, but typically it plays out differently in guys and girls. While girls tend to road trip without telling parents, take dares with drinking games, and may attempt to see how many guys they can have sex with, guys are even more aggressive with their risk taking. They may drink and drive fast, attempt feats of strength and death-defiance such as jumping off the roof of a house, and also confront enemies, gangs, or even the police. These erratic behaviors in both genders stem from no longer caring about life or living. This is severely masked depression.

Most cases of masked depression require a trained professional to identify. Once the depression is discovered and addressed, the teens may begin to show many classic signs of depression. The depression is then treated appropriately through counseling and antidepressants.

1.2F SITUATIONAL DEPRESSION

Situational depression lasts no longer than two weeks—regardless of the severity. But note that any depression can be a dark time in the lives of teens, and many times situational depression can spiral downward and become clinical depression when it lasts for more than two weeks. The following situations may trigger depression:

Loss. Including loss of hopes and dreams (e.g., loss of an expected scholarship or achievement), a relationship breaking up, friendships falling out or ending after family relocation, or friends, family members, or pets dying.

Adjustment disorder. Similar to loss, this is a circumstance that disrupts teenagers' lives. Often these experiences are labeled adjustment disorders when they take a long time to get over, such as a divorce, a move, etc. Another form of adjustment disorder is known as "complicated grief"—usually the inability to function for a long period of time, which prevents teens from resuming normal lives. Complicated grief is very difficult to distinguish from major depressive disorder.[9]

High-stress environment. Many times stress and depression go hand in hand for teens. The stress of having to perform, achieve, or make proper life decisions, along with immature coping skills, can lead teens to feel depressed.

Poverty. Many teens who live in poverty feel the hopelessness of their situation. The rising cost of living coupled with the unavailability of variables that can help them out of their situations (e.g., education, job opportunities, etc.) can cause feelings of helplessness and despair. Often these teens attempt to overcome their circumstances through inappropriate and/or aggressive means. The consequences create greater setbacks and more despair. This cycle of poverty becomes a very real concern for young teens and can lead them toward a pervasive depression.

Unhappy family and/or dysfunctional home life. Many teenagers live in homes that may be physically, emotionally, and sexually abusive;[10] these teens are candidates for major depression. Other familial dysfunctions can become part of the equation that leads to adolescent depression; they include lack of parental involvement and boundaries, marital discord, inappropriate adult coping skills, stress of blended, step-, and nontraditional family dynamics, dictatorial parenting styles, unrealistic parental expectations, etc.

Undiagnosed learning disabilities. Many teens who are unaware that they have learning disabilities often can't understand why they don't connect with school and academics. Perhaps they even work really hard—yet they usually fall short. This becomes an even darker scenario when parents and teachers hold such teens to high standards, impose consequences, and seem intolerant of these teens' situations—all of which spell a desperate, discouraging circumstance for these teens. The result is depression.

Substance abuse. Teenagers who use and abuse drugs and alcohol can develop depression that may ultimately spiral out of control. Alcohol is a systems depressant. It lowers brain function and can cause an imbalance in the chemical production and functions of the brain. Certain drugs can do the same. Stimulant drugs can also have a crash-and-burn effect that sets up the teens for depression as well.

Chronic illness. Many teens who suffer from or are diagnosed with chronic illnesses can suffer from bouts of depression. This may come from sadness that results from the inability of these teens to experience all the things a healthy teenager can. Sometimes certain medications produce side effects that lead to depression, too. Another spin on this situation is when parents of teenagers suffer chronic illnesses, leaving the teens to reverse roles, become primary caregivers for younger siblings, and live without parental involvement and nurture.

1.2G PREMENSTRUAL DYSPHORIC DISORDER

Often associated with premenstrual syndrome, PMDD is a rare but debilitating type of depression, with the same intensity as a major depression. PMDD usually occurs during the two weeks preceding a teenage girl's menstrual period and is characterized by depressive mood, anxiety, irritability, drastic mood swings, hysterics, fatigue, easy crying, and avoidance of touch. What separates PMDD from PMS is that PMDD is severe enough to hinder normal daily functions and social life. The direct causes of PMDD are not known. Some believe that it generates from an estrogen/progesterone imbalance while others point to serotonin imbalances brought about by menstruation. This depression is treated a number of ways, including through antidepressant meds, oral contraceptives that stabilize hormone fluctuation, nutritional supplements, dietary changes, and some herbal remedies.

1.3 SUICIDE

Teenagers who commit suicide usually believe that their present lives are hopelessly painful and filled with the darkest despair, and that their futures won't bring any relief, being equally dark. Death becomes the only means of escape. As mentioned earlier, suicide is among the leading causes of death among adolescents in the United States and worldwide.

Here are some important terms for us to define related to the issue of suicide:

- **Suicide.** The act of a person intentionally taking his own life. NOTE: Risk-taking behaviors that result in teens' deaths (at their own hand) are not suicides but accidental deaths. The term suicide literally means "self-murder."

- **Suicide Ideation.** Contemplative thoughts about suicide. Everyone has, at some point in their lives (maybe even during their teenage years), entertained fleeting thoughts of suicide. This, technically, doesn't qualify as suicidel ideation. For purposes of this book we'll define suicide ideation as serious contemplation, fascination, scheming, and calculating one's own death. Suicide ideation can also involve an obsession with death in general and the verbalization of suicidal thinking (e.g., "I'd be better off dead").

- **Suicide Attempt.** When teenagers willfully, intentionally, and/or purposefully behave or act in ways to bring about their own deaths, even if death does not occur. Therefore if suicide ideation precedes reckless, death-defying acts, such acts may be categorized as suicide attempts.

- **Completed suicide.** A suicide attempt that ends with the teen's death. Technically it could be called a suicide (noun) but the terminology begins to get muddy with the contemporary and cultural uses of the word. Therefore the term *completed suicide* is used instead of *successful suicide* because killing oneself is hardly a "successful" or positive action.

Suicide is often preceded by severe depression, but not all suicides are the result of depression. Some teenage suicides can be the result of suicide pacts. This is often the result of a romanticized love fantasy, or "Romeo and Juliet" effect. Teens enter suicide pacts out of idealized immaturity. When their plans, passions, and dreams seem to hit an impasse, sometimes they'd rather die than compromise.

Suicide is not always strategic. It can be an impulsive act of desperation brought on by life trauma, bad news, revenge, anger, substance abuse, psychotic disorders, or other mental health issues.

Some teens who have attempted suicide have lived to tell they never really intended to kill themselves but were overwhelmed with their circumstances.

Suicide ideation and attempts are more frequent among teenage girls than teenage guys; teenage guys have a higher rate of completed suicides. Girls tend to romanticize death and overdose on medications; guys on the other hand choose more aggressive, violent means of suicide, such as self-inflicted gunfire, hanging, or leaping from great heights. These are more lethal and less likely to be reversed once a teen has begun the act.

1.3A REASONS TEENAGERS CONTEMPLATE SUICIDE

Many reasons may seem irrational, but given the severity of depression many teens experience, ending the pain and sadness becomes the motivation, not logic and good reasons for living. Youth workers and parents need to be aware of the following motivators:

Attempting to escape situations they believe are hopeless or that they feel are trapping them. This can include teenagers who believe they're burdening someone, are physically, sexually, or emotionally abused at home, are bullied at school or are cyberbullied, etc. It's important to understand that any form of victimization tends to lead teenagers toward the belief they're hopelessly trapped. They may see death as the only means of escape.

Attempting to eliminate painful, negative feelings and depression. Teens may begin to medicate the pain by resorting to alcohol and drug use or abuse, then learn it doesn't work. They may resort to the physical pain of self-harm since the physical pain diverts their attention from the emotional pain for a short time. This respite doesn't last long, either, and the physical harm may desensitize them to greater self-harm.

The pressures of adolescence. This can include issues of popularity and rejection, body image, autonomy, future decisions, etc.

Low self-esteem accompanied by failure, sense of worthlessness, or feeling unloved or unwanted.

Loss. The trauma of broken relationships, losing a loved one and/or friends, or even the loss of hopes and dreams due to illnesses or disabilities can lead teenagers to contemplate suicide. Teenagers often lack the coping skills adults have long ago learned. In the face of extreme loss teens may not be able to navigate the trauma or have the foresight of future recovery. The suicide or death of family members or friends—even online friends—is the greatest loss teenagers face. It's also the type of loss that puts them at greatest risk of suicide.

Improper view of life. As they're still developing cognitively, teenagers tend to filter life using immature, unrealistic, and often idealized outlooks. The trauma teenagers experience, though sometimes less significant than what adults endure, is huge and no less traumatizing or painful to them. Teenagers who fail tests may experience avalanching lines of negative thinking that ends in ideations of jobless, homeless futures—and those prospects are more than they can bear. On the other hand, teens often have invincible outlooks on life—somewhere on the landscape of their thinking is a trouble-free world punctuated by drinking lattes with friends. Then when the quality of idealized lives are threatened, the trauma may be more than some teens can bear.

Improper view of death. Teens can't (or often don't) wrap their minds around the finality of death. They may romanticize it by dreaming of all the people who love them and will miss them and who'll come to their funerals and how beautiful they'll be and how wonderfully they'll be eulogized; the opposite extreme is when they view their deaths as ways of making others feel regret and sorrow for their ill treatment. This too plays itself out in fantasy with the teens imagining their adversaries weeping in regret and contrition. This improper view of death is also rooted in teens' limited ability to live in the concrete present; in other words, they believe that the intense emotion of their deaths will leave a lingering, eternal perspective on those left behind (that's also why they don't see a lot of hope when they personally suffer loss).

1.3B MYTHS ABOUT TEEN SUICIDE

Teenagers who talk about suicide never attempt suicide. When teens begin to contemplate suicide, their conversations become peppered with suicide ideation. They begin giving many verbal cues.

All teenagers who attempt suicide are clinically depressed. We've already examined the fact that while the majority of teen suicides involve depression, teens may attempt and complete a suicide for many reasons apart from depression.

Once teens determine to commit suicide, nothing can prevent it. Suicide is always preventable. Youth workers, parents, and even friends need to be aware of the warning signs. Later we'll discuss a prevention strategy.

Suicide is hereditary. This myth is often believed because some families have a history of suicides from generation to generation. While suicide isn't hereditary, there's some evidence that depression is. Some parents also pass on improper coping skills to their children. This combination of poor coping methods and depression can be a formula for suicide.

The trauma of suicide attempts will most likely deter teens from attempting suicide again. Teens who attempt suicide are at a *greater* risk for second attempts. Teens who have followed through on attempts have already learned to devise a plan and overcome fears often associated with suicide. Many times they feel their attempts were just another thing they failed to carry out—then, often second or third attempts are the lethal tries.

Teens who attempt and complete suicide often leave notes explaining their reasons. Only a small percentage of teens leave notes. Most of the time teens who attempt suicide have mulled, planned, and rehearsed the act in their minds hundreds of times. Fears, family, and friends tend to be roadblocks, but in moments of despair, pain, or anger, teens can muster the nerve to make their attempts. This often doesn't leave room for notes. This is why many families, friends, and others are left asking, "Why?"

Never use the word suicide when talking to a depressed teenager because it'll give them ideas. When friends and family notice teens are depressed, they may believe that talking about pain or suicidal thoughts might push those depressed teens over the edge. The contrary is true—avoiding the issues may cause these teens to believe everyone is unconcerned. Suicide is a desperate, last-ditch effort to eliminate pain, and the more desperate the teens become, the closer they'll be to attempting suicide. Nobody needs to give them the idea—they've already found it.

Teenagers who attempt suicide have mental disorders. Everyone struggles with depression at some point and on some level. Teens who attempt suicide feel trapped in the pain of hopelessness and despair brought about by circumstances, physiological chemical and hormonal imbalances, and negative thinking. This combination doesn't mean that there is a mental disorder.

Teenagers who commit suicide often do so without warning. This myth is widely believed because most people claim to be caught off guard by teenagers who take their own lives. On the contrary, teens who contemplate and attempt suicide leave many warning signs. Most often we're not looking for them because we don't believe anyone we know would become suicidal. Therefore warning signs are often overlooked, not taken seriously, ignored, or just missed.

1.3C SIGNS AND SYMPTOMS

There are always warning signs and symptoms present when teenagers are contemplating or attempting suicide. Often the signs are revealed forensically (after the fact by professionals) rather than remedially. People with teenagers in their lives must be made aware of the warning signs:

Symptoms of depression. These are often the primary and most prevalent signs. About 90 percent of all teenage suicides are accompanied by depression or grow out of prolonged depression. Depressed teens need to be monitored closely. Sometimes when teens appear to come out of depression, it may be that they've resolved to attempt suicide—in other words, the opportunity to escape the pain of depression may be a relief to them and paradoxically elevate their moods. Such a decision can feel empowering and can give them more energy. So if depressed teens' moods begin elevating, they need to be monitored more closely.

Verbal Cues. Teens contemplating suicide may speak about or ask questions about death and funerals. They may ask questions such as, "Does the Bible talk about suicide?" or "Do people who commit suicide go to hell?" They may make comments about being better off dead, wishing they'd never been born, or speak in terms of not having a future ("I may not be here for that"), or exclude themselves from life milestones they'd typically want to experience with their peers ("My friends will graduate this year").

Verbal cues will also accompany and explain some behavioral cues. They may talk about not needing their things anymore or ask people to take care of their pets. Verbal cues can also include teens coming right out and talking about feelings and thoughts of suicide.

Behavioral Cues. Some of these cues have already been mentioned but are worth repeating. Teens who are suicidal may engage in:

- Risky behaviors, because they believe they have nothing to live for and therefore nothing to lose. These behaviors can also include acts of recklessness that could be interpreted on the surface as acts of heroism, such as standing up to gang members at school.

- Self-harm. This may be a slow attempt at desensitizing oneself to pain and purging oneself of the fear of taking one's own life.

- Morbid obsession with death, including writing about it and artistically centering on death and dying, visiting funeral homes and cemeteries, attending wakes and funerals of people they don't know (i.e., funeral crashing).

- Drug and alcohol use and abuse. Some depressed teens plunge right into dangerous substance abuse. The mindset behind this is similar to the mindset that governs their ventures into risky behaviors—they'll do anything to eliminate the pain of depression.

- Past suicide attempts or "practice runs." This behavior is evidenced in their conversations. They may tell their friends they took five aspirins the night before "just to see what would happen." These "trial runs" are considered suicide attempts and may leave the teen disabled or permanently damaged.

Getting their affairs in order. These are also behavioral and verbal cues but they center more in the realm of death and dying. Teens who've determined to attempt suicide instinctually begin to tie up loose ends in life. Often these things are done secretly or with a low profile, so parents and adults must keep vigilant watch. Some of these cues include:

- Finishing projects, schoolwork, or favors they were asked to complete. They don't want to leave with anyone thinking badly of them or disliking them.

- Giving away their possessions. Friends and younger family members become the recipients. Teens need to understand that receiving gifts that are meaningful possessions of depressed friends is cause to contact adults.

- Canceling appointments. This is often noticed when the teen fails to make any plans past a certain date. It can also be discovered if there's an obsession with a particular date. Many times teens will pick anniversary days for their suicide days. These dates often correspond to some memorable date—e.g., the day school's out for the summer, or the day a certain hero or pop idol died. This is done out of self-protection (e.g., they may believe they'll get in trouble for not finishing school) or the desire to attach their suicide dates with already-memorable dates so their suicides themselves become unforgettable.

- Writing wills and planning funerals. Some teens will go to elaborate lengths to write their last wills and testaments or plan the things they want said and done at their funerals. This grows out of the fantasy of idealizing death. In the recesses of their minds they "can't wait to see all this happen," so they go to great lengths to plan their suicide aftermaths.

- Finalizing affairs often involves acts of vengeance. This may happen moments before the suicide. Girls tend to enact vengeance with hateful phone calls before they swallow a bottle of pills. Guys on the other hand are more violent, often resulting in murder-suicides. The warning signs are elaborate plans to carry out the vengeful acts (e.g., she may tell her friends when and how she plans to get revenge, or he may start to acquire weapons or materials to build a weapon).

Descriptive Cues. Informed, personal assessments that grow out of your relationship with suicidal teens. How well you know them will determine how accurately you can judge their cues. Descriptive cues include:

- Teens' lack of problem-solving and coping skills. If teens are deficient, then they may reach a last resort sooner than other teens.

- Impulsive behaviors. If teens have proven patterns of acting impulsively or are prone to lose control, then they may be at a higher risk of suicide.

- Attention seeking. All suicide talk should be taken seriously. Some teens are attention seekers by nature, and depression will accentuate their dramatic natures. (Keep in mind a related disorder, Munchausen syndrome, in which teens pretend to be sick or injured or intentionally harm themselves to get attention. More common in guys than in girls, this kind of harm can include breaking bones or ingesting poisons or chemicals, etc. Teens with Munchausen syndrome thrive on the sympathetic, nurturing, and compassionate attention they'll likely receive when ill or injured. Teens with this disorder sometimes accidentally commit suicide while doing self-harm.)

- Strong willed and withdrawn behavior. While this normally may be an admirable quality, it can be deadly if teens are determined to die. Add to this a propensity to withdraw, not seeking the help and support of others, and the isolation brought on by depression, and the combination can be lethal.

Situational Cues. Youth workers and parents need to be aware of the life events that shape teenagers' outlooks. Life situations that leave teens feeling helpless, trapped, or hopeless strongly factor into teenage depression and suicide. Situational cues might include loss, divorce and family dysfunction, chronic diseases, trauma, unplanned pregnancy or abortion, criminal conviction and/or incarceration, homelessness, committing immoral acts they believe are irreconcilable, etc.

1.3D SUICIDE AND GAY TEENAGERS

Adolescence is a time of sexual development and maturation. Teenagers feel sexual urges, experience physiological changes, and formulate sexual gender identities. These identities are shaped by societal norms, roles, and gender scripts. For Christian teens, navigating through the morals and biblical principles that inform sexuality are rough waters. Parents and church leaders often struggle to communicate openly and clearly about sex with teens, most often casting it in a negative light. Most teenagers wonder how sex could be so wrong when every urge in their bodies tells them it feels right. Teens also fear rejection and judgment from the church should they happen to fall or even ask the wrong sexual question.

The issue gets even more complex for gay, lesbian, bisexual, and transgendered (GLBT) teenagers. I will explore the issue of sexual orientation more in the book in this series entitled, *What Do I Do When... Teenagers Question Their Sexuality?* For our purposes, we need to realize two things: It's very likely there are teens within the scope of our ministries who are exploring or practicing gay or lesbian behavior; and it's likely that these teens struggle with fears, feelings, and a host of societal baggage that tells them they're different.

Often marginalized, GLBT teens experience harassment, threats of violence, and acts of assault, rejection, and abuse—even from friends and family members. Parents and caregivers may expel them from their homes to live on the streets. This usually forces them to quit school and often resort to criminal activity just to eat. The trauma and hopelessness many GLBT teens encounter often lead them to contemplate and attempt suicide. Sexual orientation is not a risk factor for suicide, but the pressures and traumas put on GLBT teenagers heighten their risk for suicide.

1.3E SUICIDE AND BULLIED TEENAGERS

Teens are encountering bullying and violence at the hands of their peers at near epidemic levels. Nearly 5.7 million teenagers in the United States are bullied or are bullies.[11] Bullied teens are victimized physically, emotionally, sexually, verbally, and psychologically. Teenage bullying isn't just "sticks-and-stones" name-calling that can be brushed aside; it includes slander, assault, and even assault with weapons. Many victimized teens live in daily fear of being bullied. The cruelty they experience erodes their esteem, nerves, will, and patience, creating a sense of being trapped and hopelessness. Bullied teens not only suffer the pain of depression but also the trauma of daily persecution. Suicide can seem the only way to escape the constant terror that makes an unbearable life.

Teens who commit suicide as the result of being bullied are said to have fallen victim to "bullycide." While bullied teenagers take their own lives, the event comes due to the actions of other teenagers who may never be held accountable for bullycides. Some states are seeking measures to hold others accountable in the event of teenage bullycides.

Some tormented teenagers reach the breaking point and determine to make their suicides vengeful acts as murder-suicides. Unfortunately bullied teens with this perspective are so traumatized they typically believe everyone was a part of their victimization. As a result, the vengeance can end up being massive, with many lives lost before the teens turn their weapons on themselves. Youth workers need to recognize the signs of desperation and understand what to do when teens are being bullied. Church youth ministries need to be proactive against bullying and violence.[12]

1.3F CLUSTER SUICIDES

Also called "suicide contagion," cluster suicides are characterized by an outbreak of suicide attempts or completed suicides within the same community, school, youth group, or Internet social network. Some cluster suicides are a reaction to the suicide of another teen or a celebrity. The Suicide and Mental Health Association International (SMHAI) recently found that 1 percent to 5 percent of the teen suicides in the United Stated were associated with suicide clusters. That means that anywhere from 100 to 200 teen suicides each year follow the suicidal death of another teenager. SMHAI also notes there's evidence that the rate of cluster suicide deaths is also rising.[13]

Typically this phenomenon starts with the suicide of a teenager that triggers an avalanche effect, influencing other at-risk teens to attempt suicide. This avalanche effect is called the "process of contagion." Experts have identified some factors that play into the potential of suicide contagion:

Identification. Teens with the same stressors, life situations, and depression tend to identify with the deceased victim. This empathetic connection can become so enmeshed that other teens copy the victim's "solution" or "way of escape," namely, suicide. Some teens may resort to suicide attempts using the same method, in the same place as the deceased person with whom they associate. Many times these clusters can occur among the friends and acquaintances of the deceased person. It becomes important to identify the risk factors the teens within the community share with the deceased person, starting with depression. Those teens who share common factors should be the church's greatest concern.

Imitation. The suicide of a teenager can have a pioneering effect, paving the way for others who may have been fearful of attempting suicide—i.e., one teen's suicide may empower other teens who are suffering. The completed suicide or even attempt by a teenager can give other teens courage and a form of permission to do the same.

Media. Many times information teens receive regarding a teen's suicide is from the media or public announcements. Methods, motives, memorial arrangements, sensational interviews with grieving friends and family, etc., can fuel the fire of empowerment for other teens contemplating suicide. The U.S. Centers for Disease Control and Canada's Centre for Suicide Prevention have identified the following aspects of media coverage that can promote suicide contagion:

- Simplistic explanations or reasons for suicide.
- Repetitive, excessive, ongoing reporting surrounding the suicide.
- Sensationalism.
- Reporting 'How-to' descriptions of suicide.
- Presenting suicide as a tool for accomplishing certain ends.
- Glorifying suicide or persons who commit suicide.
- Focusing on the positive characteristics of one who committed suicide.

Emotional drama. The suicide of a teenager creates a highly emotionally charged atmosphere. Adolescents are, by virtue of the developmental stage they are in, emotionally volatile. This combination can promote suicide contagion. In the book *What Do I Do When... Teenagers Question Their Sexuality?*, I warn youth workers and families to never allow open sharing during the funeral service of a deceased teenager, where teens can share their memories and testimonies of how they were impacted by the deceased. This reveals and plays into the emotional drama that naturally emanates from teenagers. (By using the word *drama* I'm not suggesting teens' pain is fabricated or any less real than adults' pain; I am indicating, however, that such sharing creates cyclical pain—it keeps teens in a state of pain. In addition, many teens may not feel grief for the deceased. The grief opens the wounds they may be carrying and becomes an opportunity for them to be openly emotive.)

For example, open sharing at a funeral service of a young teenage boy who was killed by a drunk driver ended up being hours long because countless teens stood in line to weep and give a word. Many teens started their comments by, "I really didn't know him that well, but..." Such an emotionally charged atmosphere provides empathy, compassion, sympathy, and consolation for teens who may not otherwise experience those things apart from the situation. Teens have permission to hug on, cry with, and be close to each other in pain—even if they aren't close to the person. For teens identifying with the teen or celebrity who completes suicide, this emotional atmosphere factors into the suicide contagion.

Cognitive immaturity. Adolescents often misread the finality of death and get caught up in the moment of the death. This lack of cognitive foresight can have a deadly effect. Death has a way of disrupting others' lives. Priorities shift dramatically, plans change, schools alter schedules, specialists go into high gear, the media covers and monitors, people are moved to hold vigils, etc. Even the lives of those removed directly from the deceased teen are altered for a while: They sympathize and ponder the tragedy and loss of so young a life, they monitor the news, and they may even attend a community forum or memorial. All this attention in the presence of a young person's death leaves others wanting and failing to see the finality of taking their own lives.

Other teens observe these things and fantasize about the same being done over their deaths. They get caught up in the moment, playing out scenarios of how their funerals will go, how people will mourn, console, or even be confronted with regret of past things said and done to the suicide victims. These teens fail to realize, however, that in the weeks and months to follow, the period of intense grief will eventually end. Death is final, but life continues.

The Centers for Disease Control addressed this contagious trauma with guidelines for the prevention of cluster suicides. First, community organizations (schools, churches, agencies, and businesses) should convene committees that can make the public aware and monitor teens in every sector of the community. Secondly, there should be accountability on the part of the media to not sensationalize the suicide. This media attention keeps the event in the presence of teens and serves to feed the unrealistic ideation of hurting teenagers. Carefully prepared statements from church leadership, as well as control over who the media can interview and where the media cannot trespass, are essential. Finally, counseling and ongoing support should be made readily available to teens. Those teens closest to the situation (e.g., those who attended school with the deceased teen) and teens who are at high risk for depression and suicide should be monitored more aggressively.

Understanding How Theology Informs the Issues of Teenage Depression and Suicide
| Section 2 |

2.1 THEOLOGY THAT INFORMS THE ISSUES RELATED TO DEPRESSION AND SUICIDE

As limited creatures created in the image and likeness of God, we're designed to know things only within the boundaries of antithesis—in other words, we know love in juxtaposition to hatred, light to darkness, peace to turmoil, etc. We also know the fullness of joy only as we experience the fullness of sorrow. Sorrow is part of God's design. The writer of Ecclesiastes reminds us God created everything in its time and a season for every activity under heaven, including "a time to weep and a time to laugh, a time to mourn and a time to dance" (Ecclesiastes 3:4).

2.1A THEOLOGY THAT INFORMS OUR VIEWS OF DEPRESSION

Some Christians and church leaders believe depression is directly tied to a weakened spiritual condition. This perspective is born from the belief that God disciplines us by removing our joy, prompting a saddened heart to motivate us to realign with God (as in the case of David, who pleads with God to restore the joy of his salvation—Psalm 51:11-13).

I once met with a 13-year-old guy battling severe depression (although he didn't know that's what it was). He was extremely sad and couldn't explain why, except for the fact that he thought there was something spiritually wrong with him. He explained he deeply loved God but thought God didn't love him. He told me how he read his Bible every morning and every evening, tried to find an hour each day to pray (he even showed me his prayer journal), tried to talk to his friends about Christ...and the list went on. Finally he said he didn't understand what he'd done that made God abandon him.

He was taught the wrong things. His pastor explained that depression was a direct result of a weak spiritual condition. This was doing a lot of damage. I remember thinking that I would love to be in heaven when that pastor has a conversation with Elijah, who at the height of his ministry was depressed to the point of suicide. His sorrow allowed him to experience God in a new way. And I wonder what that pastor would say to Jeremiah, called the "weeping prophet," who went through his whole ministry experience without any victory, all because God was preparing Israel for the Messiah. In the darkness of his lamentation, Jeremiah wrote some of the greatest messages of hope in Scripture. And I wonder how that pastor will respond when Jesus meets him and says, "Hi, I'm Jesus...but you can just call me Man of Sorrows," or when he encounters the Holy Spirit who says, "It's good to see you—I've been grieving over you for so many years!"

Depression and sadness are not a direct result of an impaired spiritual condition. Sorrow has a purpose in God's design and can be experienced by the most godly of God's kingdom. I do believe, however, that depression has its roots in sin, just like I believe heart disease, or tooth decay, or diarrhea is the result of a sin-stained, fallen world. Along with all creation, God desires to reconcile and redeem our depression and sadness. God can bring healing and restore our joy. But redemption doesn't mean there's always absence of sorrow. We feel sorrow over sin in the world and our own sin; we feel sorrow when someone suffers; we feel sorrow during personal suffering; and sometimes we feel intense sorrow over Christ's suffering. Just like love, sadness is complex. There's not always a single cause and effect with regard to sadness. But it has a place in God's plan and isn't always directly linked to personal sin.

2.1B THEOLOGY OF SUICIDE

For ages, churches have fluctuated on their view of and position on suicide. Some have labeled suicide as a heinous sin violating God's command not to murder; others view suicide as an unpardonable sin because the sinner has no opportunity to repent and goes to hell. Others look at suicide as a desperate result of an illness that took a life—like cancer or heart disease. The range of theological perspectives on this issue is wide.

There are no passages of Scripture that directly address God's opinion of suicide. Like most issues in life, if Scripture doesn't address it directly, then Christians look for correlating issues and passages from the Bible that can inform perspectives.

Let's look first at the issue of suicide as an unpardonable sin. Jesus said, "Whoever blasphemes against the Holy Spirit will never be forgiven, but is guilty of an eternal sin" (Mark 3:29). The Holy Spirit brings people into the conviction they need a Savior in

Jesus Christ. To continually reject that conviction in unbelief is the blasphemy of which Jesus speaks. Never did Jesus say, "If you take your own life, that's unforgivable." Our theology of atonement and salvation become vital in informing our views on suicide.

There's probably a lot of sin in our lives that we are not aware of. The good news is that God's redemption is ongoing, continuous, and powerful. With that perspective, we may conclude that suicide is sin but not beyond the scope of atonement. Another way to look at this is that suicide is the result of sin, but still not beyond Christ's reconciliation.

Suicide is a terrible thing. It can come as the result of physiological illness. It can come because a teenager lacks the hope to keep living. The responsibility of the church is not to battle over whether suicide is right or wrong; it's not to debate the eternal state of those who've taken their own lives. Our responsibility is to bring healing, hope, and restoration to the broken, painful, sick world of teenagers. The theological question lies therein: How do we bring healing, hope, and restoration to depressed teenagers?

I've encountered depressed and suffering teens who desire to escape their pain and go home to heaven. They talk about not finding any relief from their sadness and wish God would take them to be with him. This kind of talk is indicative of suicidal ideation. These verbal cues should alert you a teen is thinking about suicide. This kind of talk and thinking can come from Christian teens who love Jesus but are blinded by their pain. Therefore it's important that youth workers understand the role of hope and suffering in teens' lives. We must define hope, teach our teens to live in hope long before they encounter depression, and help them understand that suffering doesn't mean the loss of hope, nor does it mean hope will always cure suffering.

NOTE: I've outlined a more detailed look at a theology of death in *What Do I Do When... Teenagers Deal with Death?*, another title from this series.

2.1C THEOLOGY OF HOPE AND RESTORATION

Our theological perspective of hope and restoration cannot be formulated apart from how we view pain and suffering. We must consider what we believe about "hope in Christ" and how that relates to relief from suffering—physically, mentally, and emotionally. We must also be careful not to make our theology of hope so eternally focused that it becomes impotent today, directing all our attention to being with Christ in heaven. That perspective only accentuates the suffering of depressed teens and makes the prospects of death more appealing.

A good starting place in developing a theology of hope is defining the word itself. We use *hope* in so many ways to mean so many things: "I hope I get a date for the prom" or "Superman is the hope of our planet" or "There is still hope for that guy." Hope is used to categorize our wishful thinking, our future desires, and even our perceptions about someone's potential. However, hope for depressed teenagers may translate into wishing life would end. We need to help teens understand that hope for Christians lies in the fulfillment of the promises in God's Word, and that God is all about reconciliation.

Our theology of reconciliation should be rooted in the belief that God brings healing to the hurting, wholeness to the broken, and comfort to the afflicted. All of that is the result of God reconciling the world from sin through Jesus Christ. God is so intent on reconciling the world to himself that he gives us a ministry of reconciliation (2 Corinthians 5:17-20). Practically, that means we're to bring hope into depressed teens' lives by loving, listening to, affirming, empathizing with, praying for, and valuing them.

2.1D THEOLOGY OF HEALING (MEDICATIONS)

Church leaders and Christians in general have varying perspectives on the use of medication to treat depression and other psychological and emotional illnesses. Some won't take such medications, believing their use demonstrates a lack of faith in God to heal. Other Christians believe God can bring healing through medical wisdom and the use of such medications. Because church leaders are divided on this issue, many Christians are skeptical about using medications to treat emotional and psychological issues.

The medical and mental health communities have made extensive breakthroughs with research and uses of antidepressant medications. These pharmaceuticals often bring great relief and balance to the lives of those dealing with clinical depression. Some may be much healthier on medication because their bodies don't function properly without them (similar to diabetics who take insulin). Teens who take these medications can be deeply hurt by others who don't think through their theology of healing. My challenge to every youth worker is to formulate a theology of healing that intersects medical technology and the issues, illnesses, and brokenness that touch teenagers' lives.

2.2 QUESTIONS THAT DEMAND THEOLOGICAL CONSIDERATION

Rather than give you one theological perspective, my hope is that you'll carefully consider the important issues and work to develop your own theology. For this reason, I won't offer concrete answers for the questions in the section, but rather help you formulate answers—or empower you to help teenagers formulate their own answers. Some of the questions have already been put into perspective in the previous section where we raised the theological issues. Hopefully this discussion will give you more to think about as you consider your answers to each of these questions.

2.2A DOES A PERSON WHO COMMITS SUICIDE GO TO HELL?

This is a dangerous question to answer. You need to exercise wisdom before you spout off your theological opinion here. Teens who ask you this question may be looking to get over that one last hurdle keeping them from committing suicide, so your answer is incredibly important. Additionally, be cautious when teens ask this question following the completed suicide of another teen they know; you may be looking at another suicide in the making.

You may be wondering how answering this question either affirmatively or negatively may give teens a sense of resolve to attempt suicide. Consider this:

If you answer, "No, a person doesn't go to hell," or a variation of that answer, "I'm not sure—but the Bible says that those who don't believe in Christ are the only ones who go to hell," inquiring teens may be convinced they aren't going to hell—and therefore death really is the great escape from the hell they're already living in.

If you answer, "Yes, a person will go to hell because there's no opportunity for repentance for committing suicide since you're already dead," this affirms to teens who already feel worthless that they're really failures because they're planning suicides. Since they aren't thinking clearly, they may figure even their eternities are hopeless—therefore they may as well just end it. Another way I've heard this response backfire is when teens then decide they'll cut their wrists or take pills, allowing time to say a prayer of repentance before they die.

When confronted with this question, you must ask why they're asking it. Depending on the person's reason, you may answer the question entirely differently. His response may also give you indicators if he's thinking about suicide and give you an opportunity to find out what's precipitating those thoughts. You may also want to boldly ask if he's thinking about or planning to take his own life.

It is also important that you become aware of the pain and suffering that a teen may be experiencing. When a teen asks, "Does a person go to hell if they commit suicide"? That is not a time to give a theological discourse on suicide. It is not a moment to teach correct doctrine. It is a verbal cue that you should pick up on. You should explore why the teen is asking that question. In the event that the teen is not depressed and just curious may mean that the information might be passed to a friend who is struggling. You should be aware that your response could have life-threatening consequences. The best response is to say, "The church has had different perspectives on this issue because it isn't talked about directly in scripture. Besides the real question isn't if someone will go to hell if they commit suicide but why would someone be thinking of suicide?"

2.2B IS THERE SOMETHING WRONG WITH MY SPIRITUAL LIFE IF I FEEL DEPRESSED?

This is a loaded question. If you answer no, the retort may be, "Then why is God not giving me relief from my pain?" If you answer yes, the question returns the same way—only with the additional nugget: "I've done everything I can to get right with God...God must not love me." You need wisdom to discern the question behind this question—many times it's really about God's grace, mercy, and healing, as well as why God allows pain, suffering, brokenness, and even despair and death. So listen carefully. Ask clarifying questions so you know what the real issues and questions are.

2.2C ARE DEPRESSION AND SUICIDE IDEATION REALLY DEMONIC OPPRESSION?

This is a complex question you must take time to fully explore. In short the answer may be, depending on the situation, "Yes, it could be demonic oppression," or, "No, it's probably not demonic oppression." There is a spiritual reality that Satan and his demons are intent on destroying us. Therefore, can Satan and his demons confound and oppress a person to the point of self-destruction? Yes, I believe this can happen. On the other hand, Christians through the centuries have believed that demonic forces cause everything from insanity to headaches to acne. Medical advances changed some of those views—a little pill called aspirin seemed to make demons go away, for example. Obviously, we must come to a balanced perspective, and not live in a state of paranoia over demonic activity.

There's also a physiological side to severe depression. Depression is treatable with proper medications. Some who are unfamiliar with antidepressants may envision teens on meds as glassy-eyed, lethargic, and incoherent—in some ways worse off than when they were in depressive states. But given the correct doses and medication, a depressed teen can live normally—with a positive outlook, greater energy, and functioning with greater clarity. When medications are effective, it's logical to conclude that teenage depression is physiologically rooted and not from demonic influence.

If you encounter teenagers who are depressed, suggest they see counselors who can help them understand their depression and coach them on coping skills; psychiatrists who can advise appropriate medications; and youth workers or pastors who can pray for their wellness, wholeness—and against demonic forces that would come against them.

2.3 SCRIPTURE PASSAGES TO CONSIDER

Matthew 11:27-30. Jesus bids us come to him when we feel as though life's issues are overwhelming. He promises rest for our souls.

Psalm 23. God talks about restoration even in the shadow of death.

David's psalms. Even the man after God's own heart often felt the hopelessness of depression. Through songs and poems David cries out to God for strength, joy, and salvation. He longs for God to rescue him from the sorrow and fear he feels. David's experience is similar to so many depressed teens' experiences—and his conclusions and insights can restore a present hope for teens.

1 Kings 18-19. We see Elijah's depression in the light of great spiritual victory. We also see how he encounters and discovers God in a new and powerful way—while he's depressed.

Practical Action to Take When Teenagers Are Depressed or Contemplate Suicide

| Section 3 |

3.1 HELPING FAMILIES COPE WITH TEENAGE DEPRESSION

Family members of depressed teens often feel exhausted, aggravated, impatient, rejected, frustrated, angry—and even sad and desperate themselves. This can lead to family tension and conflict, which may plunge the already fragile teens deeper into depression. The following are some things you can do that will help families cope with teenage depression:

Help parents see that the frustration, rejection, and impatience they feel are often normal responses. Many times their lack of patience may be the result of some ignorance or misunderstanding about depression.

Help parents understand that a disciplinary approach to solving teenage depression may only make matters worse. I've encountered parents who bark at their depressed teens, "Just get over this! I'm sick and tired of your moping!" Some parents may resort to punishment if chores aren't done, believing their kids' lethargy and fatigue is laziness or a ploy to get out of responsibilities. They may view their teens' irritability as a form of rebellion. As depression deepens, a disciplinary hand only makes teens feel defeated and unable to please parents. Parents must be understanding and realize that punishment won't jolt teens out of depressed states. On the other hand, parents must also lovingly hold the line on boundaries, responsibilities, and expectations that are part of their teens' normal routines. This sense of normalcy creates needed security and holds teens in patterns of activity that, if otherwise ceased, would keep them in increasingly depressed states. Parents can explain to their teens that they understand it's difficult for them to stay motivated but sticking to routine expectations of everyday living will also help keep depression in check.

Help family members become educated about the illness of depression. This strategic step often becomes a crucial factor in families' coping strategies. A proper understanding of depression can often realign family members' expectations and perceptions of depressed teens.

Parents may not have anywhere to turn. Often parents or other family members may just need the empathy of someone else who understands the difficult toll that caring for depressed teenagers takes. An incredible amount of energy is required to stay patient with, hopeful for, and supportive toward depressed teenagers. It often becomes easier when parents have confidants who can lovingly support them. In addition, encourage parents to let trusted others know what's happening. Parents may avoid talking about their teen's struggles out of guilt or shame. Trusting individuals in broader support networks can help families cope better.

Sometimes it's important to remind family members their depressed teenagers are suffering, and that the family must endure it with understanding and patience. Some parents can become so impatient that quality of care is compromised as focus shifts from their teens back to themselves. The stress of living with depressed teens can cause some parents to become very needy and attention-seeking. Therefore lovingly help parents see that while they're experiencing the effects of living with depressed teenagers, their teens must be the focal point of care. Encourage parents to also take care of themselves by getting away for a while, joining a support group of other adults, planning a weekly date night, getting physical exercise, and so on.

Siblings, especially younger ones, may not understand, and get lost or overlooked in the intense focus on depressed and suicidal teenagers. Some attention on siblings can bring a lot of healing to them and become an added relief for families if they know that the church is caring for their children.

When you meet with siblings, ask them what they think of all that's going on in their families. Ask them what they think about their (depressed) brother's or sister's state. Be ready for any answer. They may express fear something bad will happen to their families. If their teen brother or sister has attempted suicide, siblings may harbor a lot of anxiety—or they may feel anger or resentment over lack of attention. They may feel guilt and hurt, thinking sibling rivalry caused this depression or suicide attempt. They also may believe they're somehow responsible, fully or in part, for their brother's or sister's emotional state. Bottom line: Help siblings understand depression.

Challenge families of depressed teenagers to seek help from support groups. These groups not only provide needed empathy, but they may also have members who've gone through similar experiences and also have a handle on healthy coping strategies. Parents can often find support groups through the counseling centers treating their teenager's depression.

Sometimes schools are aware of support groups within the school district. If your church wants to really minister to hurting teens and families, it should plan to facilitate a support group. The worst time to try to begin a support ministry for families is when those families are in the throes of pain. Support ministries must be built prior to the increased need. The old adage, "If you build it, they will come," definitely works here.

Some parents may feel guilt and shame over their teens' depression, believing they're bad parents. They may scrutinize their parenting to find incidents, principles, or decisions that may have caused their teens to become depressed. They may question their own spiritual lives and maturity, wondering if the sense of shame and spiritual stigma that depression carries in some Christian circles contributed to their teens' illness. Again, an understanding of depression can help such parents cope in far better ways.

Families must work at staying healthy by balancing their routines, engaging in healthy eating, sleeping, and exercising patterns, staying socially connected, and participating in family therapy along with their depressed teens.

Most parents and youth workers don't know the distinctions between the various mental health professionals or their specialties. Let's define some of them:

- Psychiatrist. A medical professional (an MD) who specializes in mental health issues. A psychiatrist regulates and monitors the physiological factors that play roles in the mental state of depressed teenagers but does little therapy. A psychiatrist is the only mental health professional who can administer medications. This is why a psychiatrist will often recommend psychotherapy (or counseling) with a psychologist, and a psychologist will recommend that a psychiatrist be involved in the treatment. Both are essential players on the depressed teen's treatment team.

- Clinical psychologist (also referred to as a counselor, therapist, or psychotherapist.) May be licensed and practice with a doctorate. This professional is largely responsible for the cognitive and emotive aspect of the presenting problem. A counselor will engage in honest conversation, help craft behaviors, action plans, and tools, and offer insight that can help the teen break free from the issue, or presenting problem. This is often done through consistent (weekly or every other week) sessions. It's important the therapist has a level of expertise in the field of adolescence since the complexity of that life stage must be mastered. If the therapist is not an expert nor specializes in adolescent development and disorders, then that therapist may lack the insight necessary to help in the most effective way.

- Social Worker (MSW). A counselor with either a master's degree or doctorate. The MSW tends to deal more with the systems surrounding the person with the presenting problem, meaning the teen and the family dynamic. MSWs who have special training in the area of adolescence may offer more specific and helpful guidance.

- Marriage and Family Therapist (MFT). Must have a master's degree or doctorate to practice. Area of expertise is in relational dynamics between couples and their families. Some MFTs have practices that deal with family issues exclusively while others focus only on couples' interpersonal conflicts. MFTs may be effective for family support but often may not be the best caregiver for adolescents needing individual counseling.

If depressed teens are in treatment, encourage them to stick with the treatment plan. The best way you can support depressed teens is to hold them accountable to follow doctor's orders. In addition, encourage parents to be faithful to the plan. That means monitoring medications, not missing counseling sessions, keeping an eye on daily task follow-through, etc.

3.2 DEALING WITH DRAMA IN YOUTH GROUPS SURROUNDING DEPRESSION

Misery loves company. That old saying comes true among emotionally vulnerable teenagers. Depressed teens can be the catalyst for a lot of negative drama in youth ministries. In fact, one teen's depression can yield an avalanche of emotive responses from other teens ranging from codependency to unhealthy empathizing, consuming care, and attention-seeking copycatting. Depressed teens often don't want the drama they create (e.g., the cycle of sadness, trauma, and empathy) to end because it gives them the closeness they crave. Here are some important tips in dealing with the negative drama created in youth groups:

Negativity can become an identity for an individual or a group. While it's important to recognize there's a time for sadness and grieving, there's also a time for gladness, joy, celebration, hope, laughter, and dancing. Those are the dynamics that should mark the identities of youth ministries. Even more, it's important those positive virtues be extolled and verbally proclaimed as the marks of the Christian community. If the ethos of the youth ministry becomes dampened by the drama generated by unhealthy teens, then this must be verbally challenged, and negative behaviors must be confronted.

Make your youth group one that's marked by love. Love is empathetic and sympathetic, but it also brings hope, healing, and restoration. Healthy, loving environments often quench negative drama. Some important tips on building a loving, more drama-free community include:

- Have adult leaders model healthy love responses and behaviors. Show teens how to console each other in healthy ways, how to seek out effective resources, and maybe even how to seek out professional help if the consolation is insufficient. Model and teach how to live in hope.

- Love unlovable teens all the time. Talk about this with your teens, model it from your leadership team, and expect it as the hallmark of your youth ministry. If loving the unlovable becomes the norm, it minimizes the need for dramatic attention-seeking.

- Listen. Sometimes you have to step in and confront negative drama. The unfortunate part about confrontation is that confronted teens may feel that you aren't caring or listening to their plights. But if you practice good listening skills, teens are more likely to feel loved and cared for, even in the midst of confrontation. Challenge hurting teens to talk to people who know how to listen and can mobilize effective resources for them.

- Pray for an atmosphere of love and not negativity. Prayer is one of the most effective tools in our arsenals.

Some depressed teens demand lots of attention. They can create drama by making their feelings and hurts continually central in conversations, burning out friends and adult leaders around them. Then hurting teens seek out new people unfamiliar with their plights in order to gain more sympathy and attention.

The best way to control this cycle is to create strong, loving, and clear boundaries for depressed teens, including a network of professionals and caregivers outside the youth ministry. The teens' parents or guardians, counselors, doctors, and (only) one youth leader should be part of this network. That one youth worker becomes the point person between the needy teens and the other youth leaders, if your group has them. This team of adults then keeps a watchful eye and helps redirect dramatic, unhealthy behaviors. Other leaders should be made aware that when needy teens enter high-need mode, they should be directed to the leaders charged with their care, who can often stay abreast of their treatment plans through the family.

Validate hurting teens' feelings, but dampen the drama. Sorrow and pain shouldn't be dismissed or treated lightly, but common sense and an understanding of adolescent development can give parents and youth workers the discernment to understand when hurt and pain are appropriate or attention-seeking.

Negative attention-seeking should be curbed. Adult caregivers should be assigned to hurting teens; these caregivers can offer appropriate attention hurting teens need. Crafting healthy coping strategies for hurting teens is another way to curb negative attention-seeking (e.g., logging experiences in a journal, having a single confidant to help through a negative time, or utilizing trained professionals). If teens' desire for attention supersedes their pain, then healthy strategies may be sabotaged. At that point you should confront the teens' behavior and seek to create healthy boundaries together with their parents.

Accentuate the hope we have in Christ. Teens need to know (and be reminded of) all they have in Christ—from a loving, supportive family community to an eternal future in a magnificent kingdom. The immensity of those truths will help them see that sorrow, although intense and painful, is a season compared with our eternal hope. Help depressed teens and youth groups hold on to the truth that God is continuously reconciling according to his purposes and time. Old things pass away and everything becomes new. Let hurting and depressed teens know that God also invites us into a ministry of reconciliation so we can be a part of the great things God's accomplishing in the world (2 Corinthians 5:17-20).

3.3 TIPS ON DEALING WITH TEENS WHO CONTEMPLATE SUICIDE

For youth workers, the thought of dealing with suicide intervention is overwhelming. Many believe that dealing with this issue is outside the realm of their abilities and should be reserved for mental health professionals.

While follow-up and aftercare are things professionals must be involved in, suicide intervention is most often carried out by those on the front lines with teenagers. In fact, most suicide hotlines are staffed by nonprofessional counselors with only some basic training.

If a teenager is talking to you about suicide, remain calm. If you or a parent, teacher, or counselor can be physically present with the teen, the immediacy of danger is greatly diminished. It is very unlikely for a teen to attempt suicide while someone is present with him.

First you must know how to assess how grave the situation is. I'll rank the following factors progressively. With each additional factor in the upcoming list, the graver the situation becomes:

1. **If a teenager is showing signs of suicidal ideation (listed in section 1 of this book) and talking outright about death, dying, and attempting suicide, he's in danger.** If the teenager has thought about dying or contemplated what it'd be like to be dead, this may indicate the presence of suicide ideation. You may want to ask, "Are you thinking about taking your own life?" or, "When you get real sad do you hurt yourself?"

2. **If a teenager is talking to you about death, dying, and attempting suicide, and that teenager is a fringe kid in your youth group, you hardly have a connection with her, or she's only come to a few youth group events, then she's at greater risk.** Chances are she's exhausted her network and now is looking for authoritative people she can talk to.

3. **Beyond ideation is contemplation.** This involves suicide strategies and plans. Again you should ask outright, "Do you think about how you might attempt suicide?" The more detailed the plan (e.g., knowledge of method, date, time, etc.), the more at risk the teenager is.

4. **If the teenager's actions and behaviors have set the plan in motion, he's at greatest risk (e.g., if the teen has secured pills or a firearm, written notes, given away possessions, etc.) and one step away from the attempt.** And if a past attempt is part of the teen's history, action must be taken immediately. You can acquire this information, again, by asking straightforward

questions: "Do you have everything you need to carry out your plan?" You may also ask, "Are you going to do this now, today?"

If you assess that this teen is in immediate danger, stay with him and call the police for an intervention. If you can get the teen to go to an emergency room of a hospital, do it. Many times you can talk teens into that option because they're desperate.

3.3A WHAT TO DO

You can take the following actions when confronted by a teenager contemplating suicide:

Know the warning signs. I can't stress this enough. While writing this book, a friend told me about a high school senior guy who killed himself the previous month. The boy lived three houses away from my friend. His comment was, "Absolutely nobody saw it coming." I began telling him some of the warning signs, and he began to realize that many signs were likely overlooked. Know the signs!

If teens are talking about their pain and sorrow, don't be quick to offer solutions. Listen without judging, offering advice, or lecturing. If you listen carefully you may hear more warning signs. If teens are talking about suicide, again, listen, then ask them to tell you what they're feeling. If teens are having a difficult time putting words to their emotions, use prompts such as, "If your feelings were going to become a painting, what would the painting look like? What colors would be used?" It's important you listen and validate their feelings. I realize this may sound like psychobabble, but in truth, suicidal teens typically believe they're in more pain than anyone else has ever experienced. They don't have outlets to express, release, or even feel the emotions destroying them internally—and your simple ability to listen to their emotions may be the release valve that regulates the pressure cooker of pain they feel.

Empathy comes through listening, understanding, and connecting on an emotional level to what's said rather than connecting with the content of what is said. One of the best ways you can demonstrate love to hurting teenagers is lovingly and intently listening. I've seen many suicides averted when others just took the time to listen.

Remain calm. Your steady sense of calm can bring a stabilizing peace to the situation. As long as the teen is with someone, she is much less likely to carry out her plans.

Don't ever take suicide talk lightly. Always confront teens in a timely and appropriate manner; even if you're sure they were joking, always informally pull them to the side and ask something like, "You mentioned that you may be better off dead. Did you really mean that?" They may confirm they were joking. I usually say, "Good, because I love you, and I'd never want to think that suicide is the only solution you had."

Verbalize your thoughts and concerns by asking straightforward questions. Trust your instincts and don't underestimate the fact that God may be giving you some discerning insight to help hurting teens. You're one of the best persons to determine when something isn't right with your teens. You may not be able to verbalize how you know something isn't right, but you may have some thoughts and inklings that one or more of them is at risk. Instinct tells us when this teen is behaving unusually or when this teen is covering deeper emotional trauma or when this teen is having some problems, etc. Don't be afraid to ask questions or make direct statements along the lines of what you're wondering, such as:

- "You haven't been yourself lately, and that concerns me. Is something wrong?"
- "I've noticed you've been withdrawing from your friends, and I'm concerned for you."
- "Do you ever feel like nobody cares? Do you think no one notices that sometimes you feel bad?"
- "Are you feeling so bad you want to kill yourself?"
- "Have you thought about how you would commit suicide?"
- "Do you have access to the weapon? Do you have the pills?"
- "Have you thought about when you'd do it?"

Speak in terms of the finality of death. Be persistent but gentle in your approach. Don't be afraid to use the terms *suicide, take your life,* or *kill yourself.* By the way using phrases like "kill yourself" sound blunt and aweful to say but in actuality that is the best way to concretely shift the perspective for a teen. Using the word "suicide" often romances the experience for a teenager. Teens who fantasize about death often talk about it in a less-than-final manner.

Notify family. If you've had a conversation about suicide with a teenager, you must remember that it is NOT a confidential issue. If you believe harm may be done to minors, even at their own hands, you have a duty to report it. If parents aren't the direct cause (i.e., physically, sexually, or emotionally abusive) of teens' suicidal states, then you must warn them so they can access care and keep watch over them. If parents are the cause, then you need to notify authorities such as child protective services.

Teach and model proper coping skills. In talking about the finality of death you may also mention there are other ways to overcome pain and find solutions to the problems (e.g., getting medical help, talking with a counselor, seeking the support and wisdom of others) and pledge your support. Model proper ways of dealing with sadness. Allow teenagers to actually observe you sad and how you overcome the sadness, grief, and pain in your life. Talk about that long before you're in a conversation with a teen about suicide. Show teens how you seek help from God and also from his people. Let them know that pride and fear of judgment can often get in the way of experiencing God's support through his church.

Remove lethal weapons. When you warn parents their teens are suicidal, you should ask them if there are firearms or other lethal weapons in their homes. Coach them to eliminate or lock up any weapons, including guns, knives, razor blades, box cutters, etc.

Remove all alcohol and drugs. The same should be done with prescription drugs, alcohol, and any other chemicals that can cause death.

Monitor life-situational events. Some life situations can trigger depression and hopelessness in teenagers. We've already identified many of those in the first section of this book. You should pay close attention to situations of disappointment and involving the loss of friends and talk with teens about how they're dealing with and feeling about such situations.

My friend who told me about having missed the warning signs after his teenage neighbor killed himself mentioned something else: His son is a high school sophomore. Later that evening after hearing the news, my friend went into his son's room to ask him what he was thinking and how he was feeling about the suicide. His son seemed to be doing well. My friend then said, "If you want to talk about this, I'll drop everything to talk. If you ever feel so bad you want to stop living, promise me you'll talk to me about it." His son promised. My friend did the right thing. Teens are most susceptible to suicide when other teens complete suicides.

Express love and concern for the hurting teen. Be available and unconditionally stick with them through difficult times. Tell them, "If this gets bad, you need to trust that I can get help for you even if you believe things are hopeless."

Craft a plan of action for help. If the situation is grave, get the teen to a hospital emergency room.

Encourage depressed and suicidal teens to fight shutting down. Depression tells our minds and bodies to shut down by sleeping, isolating, and introspection. Challenge teens to do things daily that counter what they're feeling and thinking, even if they don't want to. Make suggestions regarding how they can keep active. When you talk with the teens, you can ask if they're doing what they need to do. If not, have them do something immediately before the conversation continues. Also realize that these things may not be the cure for the depression but may make depression more manageable and minimize the threat of suicide. The following are some actions teens can take to combat depression:

- Talk face-to-face every day to adults or friends about the things they're feeling. Make sure they're not also struggling with depression. Misery likes company and depressed teens often gravitate toward each other (this is also why cluster suicides happen). Other depressed teens aren't the confidants needed for regaining healthy lives.

- Remain physically active. This will keep the body from becoming lethargic and weak. Physical activity helps regulate the hormonal and chemical imbalances in our systems.

- Eat regular, healthy meals. Loss of or a change in appetite is symptomatic of depression and suicide. Even if teens don't want to eat, they should be challenged to eat. Not only will this keep them healthy, it will provide needed energy.

- Regulate sleep. Have depressed teens keep a log of how many hours they sleep each day. Their cumulative sleep time should total no more than eight hours. Many times depressed teens can't control their sleep patterns, meaning they may wake up in the middle of the night and stay awake tossing and turning for hours; then they may supplement by napping later in the day. They should work hard to eliminate the napping and keep the cumulative sleep time to eight hours. This may require teens to utilize alternative actions such as engaging in a project or hobby, taking a cold shower, exercising, etc., to keep them from sleeping.

- Stay connected and engaged with friends. Social connections are vital. Some teens withdraw because they don't find joy in being around friends or engaging in other activities they once loved sharing with their friends. They must realize that this is depression talking, and they can't submit to it. Remaining engaged can help them stay connected to normalcy. It may even bring back some joy.

- Keep a daily routine and stick to it. Teens who plan to attempt suicide tend to resist any scheduled routine or future plans. In fact, they may work hard to change and cancel future events because they're planning to not be around. This is how they get their affairs in order. Asking teens to keep written schedules, therefore, will make it difficult for them to get caught in the behaviors common to depression and suicide ideation.

- Be proactive about making suicide difficult. Depressed teens should plan to be accountable. That means continually communicating with their parents or guardians about what they're doing and why they're doing it. Teens must also be challenged to eliminate from their environments all weapons, chemicals, drugs, alcohol, and any other objects that could be used as a means of taking their lives.

- Have an "out-strategy." This is a plan made in advance to keep teens from spiraling downward into suicide. Teens should be challenged to promise that if they begin to entertain thoughts of suicide they'll call people who can help them out of their suicidal downward spiral. These people are agreed-upon individuals who know how to deal with the teens' depression and can be available to mobilize resources to get them stabilized. The list of agreed-upon people can include family members, clergy and youth workers, counselors, teachers, and doctors. If there are no such people available, then the teens must agree ahead of time to go to a hospital or call the police for intervention.

- Get out in the sun. Have teens spend some time outside, even if it's a 30-minute walk. If the weather is bad, then suggest they see a doctor regarding the use of light therapy.

- Consistently follow through with treatment. Teens will often fight taking medications, make excuses about not liking a therapist, disregard clinical directives, etc. Regardless of the excuse, depressed and suicidal teens should follow through with treatment. They may not see immediate results, but their persistence will pay off in the long run.

- Serve others. Depressed and suicidal teens should be challenged to serve others. Serving in a soup kitchen, doing tasks for those who are disabled or shut in their homes, visiting lonely people in retirement homes, volunteering in hospitals or orphanages, or participating in community after-school programs often helps hurting teens keep a proper life perspective. Such activities also take the focus off themselves and make them more other-centered.

Refer teens to professional counselors. Depressed and suicidal teens need more than supportive people in their lives. Every youth worker needs to be able to identify counselors, therapists, social workers, and psychiatrists in their communities who are trained in working with teenagers. Build a referral base of qualified Christian mental health professionals before you need them so when the time comes, they'll be there for you.

I've met parents and pastors who wouldn't seek (and even refused) professional help for suicidal teens because they didn't have immediate access to Christian mental health professionals. But the goal of a non-Christian therapist in a crisis intervention is the same as the goal of a Christian therapist: To get the teenagers stabilized and keep them alive. In an emergency, it doesn't matter if help and intervention is carried out by Christians or not. There will be ample time for selecting Christian therapists post-intervention. Youth workers can also encourage teens and their families to get into group support with others who have gone through similar experiences. This may also be a good ministry for your church to establish.

3.3B WHAT NOT TO DO

Don't underestimate teenagers. In November 2008, a 19-year-old guy committed suicide online while nearly 1,500 people watched. Beforehand he posted suicide notes online and talked about his method of suicide in a video blog. He bantered back and forth with many in a Web chat who either encouraged him to "do it" or rationalized the pros and cons of quality living. Then he swallowed a bottle of pills and lay on his bed while the video kept streaming. Several hours later the police were notified and rushed into his room—but he was dead. As the victim's computer video camera was left on, their rescue attempt was also streamed live over the Internet. Despite the tragedy of this event, many believed it was all a hoax. The people who took part in the taunting, bantering, philosophizing, and so on underestimated the victim and disregarded the seriousness of his suicide threat.

By the same token, teens who joke about suicide should be subject to the same line of action as someone who is actually serious about suicide. These teens should be confronted, have family notified, be taken to a hospital if their plans are elaborate, and talk with a professional counselor. If the teens' joking is elaborate, then it would seem there's some issue driving this behavior that merits professional attention. Don't ever underestimate teens' threats, cries for help, or even jokes.

Don't try shock treatment. In other words, don't say things like, "Enough with the self-pity, why don't you just go ahead and do it?" or, "What's stopping you? Are you afraid you might screw it up?" or, "That would be just like you to ruin a lot of people's day." Some believe that if they attempt paradoxical interventions, then the teens will be "shocked" out of their suicide ideation. But this kind of shock treatment is never appropriate when dealing with teenagers whose perceptions about life and death are clouded by depression.

Don't argue the pros and cons of living. Suicidal teens have already done this at great length, and having pondered this argument, they've come to the conclusion life isn't worth living. Your argument may be patronizing to them and may add more pressure, further entrenching suicidal teens in decisions they've already made.

Don't assume time heals. Many people believe that teenagers who talk about suicide are caught up in the drama of the moment and they'll suddenly experience an emotional shift that will bring them away from suicide ideation. These people usually end with advice like, "Things will look better tomorrow." Unfortunately if depressed teens have the plans and means to carry out suicide attempts, they've already pondered this for quite some time. Time is not the healer of this wound. Parents often mistakenly take this approach when their teens experience the loss of broken relationships. Some adults don't see the intensity of teens' depression because the issue seems small to them in the overall context of life. But each teen deals with loss differently. Some cannot cope with the pain well and allow it to spiral out of control in their minds. Bottom line: Time may indeed heal their wounds—but only if they're able to maintain perspective and not take aggressive action to end their own lives.

Don't make false promises. "Life will get better" or "This problem will pass in a week or so" or "God's going to take away your sadness soon" or "I promise to never disappoint you if you'll stay alive." These only breed false hopes that can crush teens when they're not realized. Timetables, pain thresholds, expectations, and perspectives are skewed in the lives of depressed and suicidal teens. Your promises may be misinterpreted and held to as an "only" hope. When not realized, teens may become more deeply entrenched in their determination to take their own lives.

Avoid pat answers and clichés. "You're young, talented, and beautiful; you have everything to live for." Such clichés feel hollow in the ears of suicidal teens. Their life experiences tell them they have nothing to live for, so your words sound disingenuous—like a used-car salesperson trying to close a deal. Some Christian truths can also sound like platitudes to depressed teens. It's important you speak the hope of Christ into the lives of these hurting teens, but you need to say it with sincerity and without cliché.

Avoid trying to thoroughly correct theological perspectives. Hurting teens may have warped theologies. They may say they're afraid to commit suicide because they'll go to hell. Or they may say they have a burden too difficult to bear, so suicide is the only option. This isn't a time to correct theology on the eternal destination of suicidal teens or the theology of the purpose of trials and God's provisions of escape. Instead listen, feel, empathize— then offer hope...not theological discourse. Too many Christians believe that correct theological views are the most important things to maintain, but in the case of hurting, suicidal teens, they're most definitely not. Care and support are what is needed now. Correct theology can come later.

3.3C INTERCEPTING A SUICIDAL TEEN THROUGH TECHNOLOGY
Youth workers and some parents have access to social networks

such as Facebook, Twitter, and MySpace. These are places where you can find out the emotional states of many teens. Some say things on social networks they'd never say publicly. In addition they may post their real feelings online but hide them in real life.

I'm not suggesting that parents should snoop or spy on their teens. This type of activity can breed strong mistrust between teens and parents. But I do suggest that if parents believe their teens are depressed and may be contemplating suicide, they should check every avenue that could offer insight so help may be secured if necessary. Of course, such action should be carried out with finesse and loving concern, but I've encountered too many parents who find their teens' suicide ideations posted online after it's too late to intervene. Once again, this monitoring should be done only to verify the suspicions parents may have regarding their children's suicide ideation and depression.

Watch postings on social networks. Teens often leave cues on Twitter or Facebook. They may make comments about how terrible their lives are or about wishing they were dead. The more frequent, intense, and pervasive these kinds of statements become, the more cause for alarm.

Follow their friends. Depressed teens may not post alarming cues on their status bars or in their profiles, but they may say alarming things to their friends through posted comments on friends' pages or walls.

Read their blogs. Teens who plot their demise often leave cues in blogs. The planning of a suicide starts out as a fantasy, then can gain momentum by becoming a concrete plan. Teens begin writing along those same lines. They may post creative writings—essays, poems, or stories with death and dying themes. As their plans develop these teens may blog about methods of death, their last desires, insights about and reasons for suicide, justification for self-inflicted death, etc. If they have vengeful motives, these may also be revealed in their blogs. Teens who plot murder-suicide vendettas often tell about their plans in blogs or online postings.

3.3D DUTY TO WARN

When the lives or safety of teenagers is threatened, youth workers have a responsibility (and in many cases, a legal responsibility under penalty of law) to seek proper resources and notify appropriate authorities who can help those teens. This is called a "Duty to Warn," and it means that if any harm may come to a minor or to others at the hands of a minor, then adults with that information are responsible to warn, appropriately.

Youth workers are ethically bound to warn about potential teen suicide. While there are no laws mandating this reporting (as with suspected child abuse cases, for example), youth workers can be liable in civil suits if teenagers complete suicides and the youth worker had knowledge of the teens' intentions. Thoughts and plans of suicide are never confidential matters, and they require youth workers to take action.

Suicide ideation and verbalization should quickly be brought to the attention of the parents of the teens in question so they can secure proper professional help immediately and keep a watchful eye on their kids. Tell the parents the information revealed to you. If you believe the danger is imminent, suggest that the parents take their teens immediately to a hospital emergency room for evaluation.

The only time you shouldn't notify parents is when you have reason to believe that the behaviors of the parents have precipitated the suicidal ideation in the teenagers, and that the teenagers may be in more danger if their parents are notified. In that case your actions should include notifying your state's child protective agency regarding the parents' behaviors.

For example, a teen may not want you to notify his parents about his suicide ideation because his depression is the result of being abused by his parents. In that case, notifying parents may make your teen feel more trapped in his abusive situation, and he may resort to suicide as a spontaneous means of escape.

Duty to warn can also mean you warned the parents by getting their involvement in an intervention, or that you warned a medical doctor by bringing the teenager to an emergency room. This statement always bears repeating: Suicide is not a confidential issue.

Unfortunately some youth workers become trapped when they make suicide a confidential issue. This often happens to youth workers with a warped sense of confidentiality. Many times this grows out of youth workers' need to be needed. They promise confidentiality they cannot and should not deliver, or they end up underestimating the gravity of the depression and suicide ideation and not saying anything. They believe they're qualified to handle these situations because of their relationships with depressed, suicidal teens. The following are some boundaries youth workers can set and practice well in advance:

Never get backed into a corner. Teens should know up front you'll always respect their confidentiality except in cases where harm may be done to someone. Don't tell teens that everything they say to you is confidential—that's irresponsible and lacks maturity and wisdom. Blanket confidentiality binds the hands of the youth worker to mobilize effective help for the teen and makes the youth worker seem untrustworthy when confidence must be broken.

If teenagers feel as though they can't live within that boundary and decide to walk away without telling you what they intended to tell you, be content to live within that boundary. Too many youth workers can't stand the fact that a teen may choose NOT to tell them something, so they compromise their boundaries by agreeing to keep confidentiality. This will either put youth workers in a position to be held accountable (and possibly prosecuted) for the information they withheld, or it makes them liars if they report according to mandated laws.

If the teenager insists the information be kept confidential, ask him what he expects you to do with the information he wants to disclose. Often the teen will say he wants you to help him make a decision or offer advice about a situation. Lovingly help the teen understand there's no wisdom in asking for help if he doesn't allow others to help on their terms.

Reaffirm how much you value the teen and let him know that some issues require you to take nonconfidential action out of love and concern. Ask the teen to trust you to do what's best. Affirm you'll keep confidentiality whenever possible and seek God's wisdom and discernment to guide your response.

Help teens see that suicide can't be a confidential issue. Like some youth workers, often teenagers are backed into corners by friends who threaten suicide. Help these teens realize that good friendship means keeping their friends alive. It's far better for their friends to live and be angry with your teens for breaking confidentiality than for your teens to live in the regret of not taking action or telling someone. Teens need to know that suicide is not a confidential issue.

3.3E SUICIDE INTERVENTION STEPS

I've given you many tips on suicide prevention. But what do you do when a teenager tells you face-to-face he's planning to shoot himself tonight? What if you get a phone call from a teenage girl who says she's just swallowed a bottle of sleeping pills? These circumstances call for immediate intervention. The following are a few steps you can take:

Stay with teens if you're talking face-to-face. Remember that your presence greatly reduces the chance of them attempting suicide.

Talk them into getting some help. Obviously they want it; otherwise they wouldn't have sought you out. Remind them that you'll be available to them through this hard time, but those more qualified than you are needed to help them through the complex feelings they're facing.

Notify family members to come and get their teens and take them immediately to the hospital for care and evaluation. Stay with the teens until family arrives. As noted previously, teens often contemplate suicide when the abuse in their homes is more than they can handle—and in those cases, contacting parents is likely to do more harm than help. As an alternative, take these teens directly to the emergency room of the hospital. The staff there will make arrangements to notify parents and authorities if necessary. Most states have statutes that allow minors to seek emergency medical treatment without parental consent if their life and health is at such risk that treatment should be administered without delay. If you find it difficult to take such teens to a hospital without parental consent, then notify emergency services by calling 911.

If family members can't be reached, take the teen immediately to a hospital. Mental health practitioners can evaluate them there and proper steps will be taken for their care.

If your teens are hostile, resistant, or run from you, call emergency services at 911 and seek intervention from the police or paramedics.

If teens tell you of their suicide plans over the phone, find out where they are and call emergency services at 911 for intervention. Some teens may call you, for instance, after they've already taken pills. So in addition to finding out their location, ask them what they have taken and how much. It's also important to know if they used alcohol to wash down a medication.

If you believe talking with suicidal teens has helped, and the imminent danger of suicide is past, you should still:

- Contact parents so they can keep a watchful eye on the teen.
- Make arrangements to meet with the teen in the next couple of days. As noted previously, teens who determine to

commit suicide often won't commit to future plans. As a part of getting and keeping their affairs in order, they cancel appointments and refuse to make appointments they cannot keep because they believe they won't be alive to keep them.

- Assist and encourage teens and their families to seek professional help. The key is to refer, refer, refer. While you're qualified for a suicide intervention, you need a professional to do an assessment and administer treatment for a suicidal teenager.

3.4 DEALING WITH LOSS THROUGH SUICIDE

3.4A HELPING FAMILIES WHO'VE LOST TEENS AFTER SUICIDE

One of the reasons the death of a child is so incredibly difficult to process is because it defies natural life expectancy. Parents never plan or expect to outlive their children, so when a child dies (regardless of the child's age), the parent's grief is great. When death comes through suicide, the grief process becomes more complex.[14] There are specific ways youth workers can help families who lose teenagers through suicide:

Give support to those dealing with the trauma of finding a deceased teen. Many times a parent or sibling finds the body. Witnessing the scene of a suicidal death is often very traumatic, especially if violent methods are used. Images of a hanging body, a gunshot wound to the head, and slashed wrists don't leave anyone's mind very easily, but that's especially true of parents and siblings. Many times they'll need or want to talk about this. It's understandable to want to avoid such conversations with survivors, but your ministry may require you to fill that role. This may also be true if a teenager enters the scene of a parent who's committed suicide. Shock, fear, and guilt can sometimes keep others from talking about what they witnessed. But once they break through these issues, they may need to process their pain and trauma with others. If they choose to do that with you—just listen. You don't have to respond, give answers, or help them understand—you only need to listen, empathetically understand, and console.

Encourage families to avoid blame. Many times parents will replay in their minds confrontations they had with their deceased teens, scrutinize their parenting, retrace their actions, and attempt to recall their conversations to see what they did wrong or where they missed the mark. They may say things like, "If only I had..." or, "I should have never..." This type of self-blame is a normal response. We all take personal inventory upon the death of a loved one.

But such self-blame can spiral out of control and become unhealthy if it impedes the healing and recovery process. Parents should talk to a professional counselor to work through feelings of blame and regret.

Some parents also may blame each other, tearing apart their relationship and destroying their marital bond. Blame is often at the center of why many couples separate and divorce after the death of a child.

We must try to support parents by helping them realize that feelings of blame are normal, but are not a healthy coping skill. The surfacing of blame and guilt may also prompt a family to be open to seeking professional counseling.

Help families through the difficulty of what to tell others. Suicide carries a stigma. Families of teens who've committed suicide may feel they're being judged or labeled as dysfunctional. So not only do they suffer the traumatic loss of a child, but they also experience the shame of the experience. This leads them to wrestle through the discomfort of not knowing what to say. Anything short of the truth can also leave people confused and wondering.

Three months into my first youth ministry job I received word a boy in our youth group was killed in an auto accident. I expected to meet the family at the hospital, but they didn't want anyone to come. There was no report in the news of a fatal accident, nobody saw a wrecked car or could get a straight answer as to where the accident occurred. The casket was closed, the funeral was quick and small, and the family avoided any talk of the "accident." To this day, I don't know what happened, but I suspect that the shame of a suicidal teen may have driven a family to do whatever they could to save face. This approach backfires because family members never get the healing they need. Therefore, help families know that depression is an illness that can take lives. Help move them past the shame by embracing their grief and being a gracious and safe "place" for them. Be an advocate on behalf of a family who suffers loss from a suicide by openly battling the stigma and judgment that can follow the event. In doing this you model to your church family that its collective role is to be loving, restoring, healing, and gracious to those in grief and pain.

Understand grief. Human beings move through stages in the grieving process. Sometimes the stages overlap. Sometimes people vacillate between stages. And sometimes people move quickly through a stage, where others may become fixated on one stage. In the event of suicide the stages can take on some of the following distinctions:

- **Shock or denial.** This often begins with the accompanying trauma of finding the deceased. Parents can be shocked all the more because they didn't pick up on the signs or recognize the symptoms and cues. Denial can play itself out in the shame that sometimes accompanies suicide. Then the normal part of denial and shock typically kick in, such as having visions or dreams they saw or heard their child or commenting they still wait for them to walk through the door, confirming temporarily that the experience "must have been a bad dream."

- **Anger.** Many times grieving parents will direct anger at themselves because they didn't prevent the suicide or see the warning signs. They may be angry about things they said, did, or didn't do. They may then become angry at others, thinking they could've done more as well. You may even bear the brunt of this anger. Some parents lash out at youth ministries, churches, and youth workers for what they perceive as lack of care. This blame and anger can be devastating for youth workers who may also be going through the grief of losing teens who were part of their ministries. They may also become angry with the deceased teenagers for not seeking help, putting the family through this pain, for leaving them, etc. This can become a very difficult anger to process because it's often repressed (in that people believe it's wrong to be angry at a dead person), and then there may be no resolve.

- **Bargaining.** While it's hard to bargain for the life of a deceased teenager, families often bargain with God for the protection of other siblings. This can also manifest itself in overprotectiveness or smothering of younger siblings of the deceased teen. Parents may not let them go out anymore; they may accompany them to events and wait for them when they didn't before; they may constantly call or check in to be assured that everything is all right; they may also constantly want surviving siblings to be in their sight or care. Fear becomes the driving force of this bargaining stage.

Some Christians bargain with God for an understanding of why this happened to this teen and why he had to endure this pain. So they bargain for peace, consolation, and joy even though they despise that they may feel joy while their deceased child clearly didn't.

- **Depression.** Sometimes parents become depressed while grieving their deceased children. The depression may become so great they may even attempt suicide themselves—despite the fact that they know firsthand the extent of trauma, anger, etc., the suicide of their children created. NOTE: The suicides of their children have almost the same effect on parents as cluster suicides have on other depressed or at-risk teens. Their children's suicides give them courage to die—some parents even imitate their children's suicide methods as a means of reclaiming some connection to them.

- **Acceptance.** At some point family members begin to accept the teenager's death. They may come to terms with the suicide and even advocate for suicide prevention. Some can lead support groups, others volunteer to work suicide hotlines. Most just resolve to get back into the normalcy of life.

Expect desperate attempts to understand why this happened. Parents, siblings, and friends may go through this phase. As noted previously, parents often spend countless sleepless nights wondering how this could have been prevented or how it could have happened. If they don't find resolve, they replay the life, conversations, situations, conflicts, etc., involving their children. They may seek out pastors (even leaders of other religions) to help them formulate answers. They may engage in conversations with the deceased teenager's friends in hopes of finding out some other clue that might have been missed. As you might expect, such a tactic can often scare these friends or make them feel responsible in some way for their friend's death. This is often why a support group is necessary. Encourage grieving parents to get into support groups so they can discover how others have walked through this darkness.

Talk about the deceased teenager. So many times in the tragedy of a suicide, others assume they shouldn't talk about the deceased because of the pain surrounding the suicide. They're afraid that if they bring up the deceased, then it will trigger too much pain for the family. In reality this avoidance makes the family feel judged, or that everyone is avoiding the obvious by walking on eggshells. The obvious, to a hurting family, is that someone they love is gone, and they need others' support. Don't be afraid to talk about your memories of the teen. Don't be afraid to use the deceased teen's name. Don't be afraid if family members weep when you mention the deceased teen. They are weeping anyway—and often. Family members would rather be allowed to cry than feel as if they have to hide it.

Remember that anniversaries, birthdays, and holidays will be difficult for a grieving family. Often their anticipation of the event may be more difficult than the actual event because they fear they'll fall apart or that the grief will become too great to handle. Some families have difficulty with holiday traditions because of the missing person. So encourage families to continue the traditions by adding something like lighting a candle preceding the tradition, in memory. Or encourage families to resolve their grief all the more by generating new traditions. Traditions surrounding the event or holiday should be talked through, retained in memoriam, or modified to form new traditions. Youth workers and the church can minister to families who have lost a teenager to suicide by remembering as well. Keep the birthday of the deceased teen in your computer or PDA—then when the date comes up in reminders, call the parents and let them know that you still think of them and pray for them. In the weeks and months following the suicidal death of the teen, visit the family frequently. Many families feel suddenly abandoned by their teens who commit suicide; then they feel a repeat when all care goes away after the first couple of weeks have gone by.

Help families regain as much normalcy to life as possible, especially if other siblings are present. Families (parents) may need to be challenged to go through the motions of normal life even if they don't feel like it. Younger siblings may not understand or feel the longer-term complications of grief, so getting them back to soccer practice, playing games, and experiencing the routines of normal family living is essential. This also helps adults from falling further into depression.

As mentioned, parents may become overprotective of other siblings for fear of losing them. Many times parents don't see this, so it may take a lot of wisdom, finesse, proper timing, and coaching to help them realize they're smothering their other children. You may need to advise parents to seek professional help to overcome the fears causing this behavior.

Help the family with funeral arrangements. The trauma of a suicide can be so great that planning a funeral and all the details that accompany it can be placed on a back burner. Families in this situation then get suddenly thrown into the waters of making huge decisions regarding death rites, wakes, services, funerals, and memorials. In addition, they may have questions about the church's position regarding the suicidal death of a teenager. These questions may create a lot of anxiety because parents may have preconceived notions regarding the topic. Fear keeps them from asking if they can have the funeral in the church, or if the pastors or priests will officiate the funeral. Their fear of the answers may immobilize parents from thoroughly planning a funeral, or it may lead them to make decisions they wouldn't have liked.

A youth worker could immediately offer the support of the church and help with the planning of a funeral and memorial. This involves a lot of work and preparation. The book in this series, *What Do I Do When... Teenagers Deal with Death?*, provides a number of checklist points and a sample program from a teenager's funeral service. If a youth worker is asked to officiate the funeral service of a teen who completed suicide, she should carefully construct what she should and will say so the family isn't embarrassed or shamed. A youth worker should also consider there are many in pain and that the pain of depression may have brought everyone to this place. A message of hope and healing becomes the appropriate response.

Shield the family from the media. Often the suicidal death of a teenager can attract media attention. A family may need to be assisted in writing a press release and appointing a spokesperson to represent the family. That point person should field all inquiries and protect the family from the persistence of the media.

Encourage the family to seek professional counseling and a support group. This is worth repeating: Encourage hurting parents to get professional help and support.

3.4B HELPING TEENS WHO'VE LOST SOMEONE TO SUICIDE

It's important you be slow to speak. Allow teens to talk about their feelings. They may be very confused, angry, hurt, and sad. The suicidal death of teenage friends creates a ball of emotional yarn that's difficult to untangle. Listening is the tool to help the yarn knot begin unraveling.

Allow teens to ask questions. You may be surprised by how profoundly deep and theological teenagers' questions can be during a difficult time following a suicide. They may ask about the salvation of a friend who committed suicide or why God didn't relieve their friend's pain. They may question the goodness of God or maybe even God's existence. This isn't a time to correct their theology—it's a time to live through it with them. Focus on getting past the grief. Don't try to answer all their questions—most of the time you'll sound like you're giving canned answers. Realize that during the pain of trauma, no answer will truly satisfy. So be patient. Later when questions surface, help teens find the answers to their questions.

Share memories of the deceased. This is a very healing exercise to do with hurting teens. Ask them, "What's the most fun you ever had with _____?" or, "What will you always remember about _____?" Don't be afraid if this provokes tears.

Help them experience closure. Some teens say they wished they had said or done something while their friend was alive. Encourage them to follow through with their wishes by writing a letter or saying what they would have said by imagining their friend is there. If it's something they wish they had done, have them identify a representative (the deceased's younger sibling, parent, significant friend, etc.) and carry out the action. You may need to help teenagers be sensitive to grieving family members. This type of activity may be best done after they've had ample time to mourn their loss.

Help teens manage the changes death brings to their lives. The loss of a friend can disrupt teens' routines, their social contexts, and even their family schedules. Have teens talk through their perceptions of how things will change. Challenge them to think about what they plan to do and what they may need to make the changes.

Model healthy grief and coping skills. Be candid. Tell kids what you are thinking and feeling. Let them see—and participate in—your sorrow. Tell them this raises questions you find frustrating and unanswerable in your mind, too. Show them what you do to overcome grief and how you plan to continue to live life in a healthy manner.

3.4C DEBRIEFING YOUR YOUTH GROUP AFTER THE SUICIDE OF A TEENAGER

Brief all your church and youth leadership ahead of time. Fill them in regarding the details and information that will be shared with the group and the strategy for the youth group debriefing.

Communicate well with parents. Let parents know the time and place where you'll meet with the youth group. It's usually best to suspend the normal programming on the night your youth group usually meets. Do this right after the death of the teen. Communicate your plans to parents via email, posting on your ministry's Web page, or phone chain. Let parents know that you'll be dealing with the death of a teenager and encouraging teens to follow up with parents after the meeting. Let parents know your strategy and hopes for the youth group debriefing. Give them the facts and allow them to be involved if they desire.

Let parents know this meeting will give teens opportunities to candidly process their thoughts and feelings with each other. To create this kind of environment, you're recommending that parents don't participate, but that they help by following up with their teens after the meeting. Tell parents you'll have a crisis team available to teenagers at the meeting and in the days following. If a parent insists on being at this meeting, allow the parent to do so by remaining on the periphery of the meeting and ready to assist if you need help. In your communication, coach parents to be sensitive and available to their teens later in the evening, to drop off and pick up their teens before and after this meeting, and to be available to grieve with and listen to their teens, to acknowledge the sorrow of death with them, and to monitor their own teenager's well-being.

Give teens the facts as allowed by the deceased parents. If the word is out that the death of the teen was self-inflicted, and the parents of the deceased teen are comfortable with you talking about that, then address the nature of suicide and the issues that may lead one to commit suicide. This is a good time to do some preventive care. Tell teenagers they should talk with trusted adults who can help them about the things they're going through and feeling. Do this in pointed, well-stated comments rather than making it an opportunity to lecture on suicide. As much as possible keep the focus on the grief of the teenagers left behind. The facts you can also give should include time and date of funeral, ways they can minister to the family, and things that teens can do to direct their grief in positive directions (e.g., creating a memorial Web page, writing stories, creating a photo wall or collage, etc.).

Have a crisis team available. Every youth ministry should have a crisis team trained to aid teenagers as needed. Often the suicidal death of a teenager is impetus to formulate such a team. These people should be at your debriefing to lend their expertise immediately, if needed. Members of this team should include counselors, teachers, medical personnel, and pastoral caregivers.

Keep a watchful eye on teens who are depressed and at risk of cluster suicides. Parents need to be notified to keep watch on their teens if they're at risk.

Allow teens to ask questions. Answer any questions they may have. Acknowledge you may not be allowed to answer some questions because of the privacy afforded to the family, because of privileged information, or because you don't know the answer to their questions. If theological questions arise, answer them to the best of your ability without going into a long theological discourse. Also remember it's okay to acknowledge you don't know or understand how to answer a question or how your theology fits the situation.

Let teens express their thoughts and feelings. Allow plenty of time for teens to talk about what they're feeling and their memories as well as share stories and personal struggles that arise from this situation. Be aware you may experience a range of emotions from laughter to hysterical crying.

Allow teens to stay as long as they like and continue to talk. This is often when you need to have your crisis team more available. Many teens who could be at risk may tend to become overwhelmed and stay behind. Others may find this a more intimate time to hang with friends.

After the initial meeting, create times and opportunities for teens to be together without agendas or programs. Encourage parents to have teens in their homes. Encourage teens to organize their own meetings. They need a lot of hang out time when death hits a youth group, especially when it's a suicide. The community and connectedness can heal and fill the gap left by death.

3.4D DEALING WITH PERSONAL GRIEF

When a teenager dies suddenly—whether by suicide or not—a youth worker usually needs to go into helper mode and holds the role of "minister" to everyone around. This often doesn't immediately allow much room for personal grief. Without question, youth workers are deeply affected by the loss of teens under their care, especially when it's a suicide. The following are some guidelines:

Don't hide what you're feeling. Many people believe that if they show their emotions, then they'll be perceived as a weak helper—and often that "strength" is communicated by remaining emotionless. But what's really communicated by not showing genuine emotion is apathy and lack of concern. Remember at the death of Lazarus, Jesus was moved to tears—so don't be afraid to grieve, too.

The suicidal death of a teenager may make you question a lot of things, just like your kids. Therefore find a confidant who'll hear your questions and make a safe place for you to ask those questions. Realize that some of your questions may not have satisfying answers.

You may question your effectiveness. Often youth workers say the same things parents do. They wonder why they didn't see signs, or how they missed the signals. They wonder why the teen didn't come to them with their problems or issues. You need to remember that blame doesn't change the situation.

You may get blindsided by the grief and rage of a parent. We already described the rage and blame parents feel when they lose their teenagers to suicide. If directed at you, their verbal abuse can be devastating, especially as you're also experiencing grief and questioning your effectiveness. Grieving parents may say things that are irrational in the heat of the moment. So, if you get blindsided by rage:

- Don't take it personally. This will be difficult to do because the attack may be aimed directly at you, your work, or the perceived quality of care you give teens. Remember it is parents' grief and rage that are speaking. Also remember that their blame is often displaced against the rage they feel for themselves, believing they were ineffective.

- If this verbal lashing is difficult for you to get past—DON'T LEAVE THE MINISTRY—get help. Seek out a mentoring pastor who can share ministry struggles with you and how those pains were overcome. Talk to a counselor who can help you get past the trauma of the suicide and the accusations of blame.

- Don't try to reconcile the relationship, at least not for a long time. Realize that grief will still get in the way and a parent may grieve for many months or longer. You may also determine not to reconcile the relationship but live in a reconciled state; this means you can be forgiving and loving and engage the grieving parent without shame, guilt, or hostility. It means you can live in the understanding this terrible situation has deeply wounded a parent who may not be able to get past his perspective.

Take some time to heal and grieve. It may be good for you to take some time off and meet with a spiritual director or friend who can minister to you. Find a place of refuge and relax, journal, grieve, or find relief. On the other hand realize you may not need spiritual solitude—but you might need fun! In that case, give yourself permission to take time to do something fun and exciting. This may be the way you reconnect with the joy of Christian living.

3.5 PREVENTIVE MEASURES AGAINST CLUSTER SUICIDE

The Centers for Disease Control has issued a community plan for the prevention and containment of cluster suicides. This plan is great—but it needs an initiator. Who better to initiate this community plan than youth workers who love and care for the teenagers in their communities? I've listed in the resource section of this book the Web site that outlines the plan. Some of the finer points of making this plan work:

If you're going to initiate this plan, you need to act quickly and decisively. Don't wait around to see if some other organization is taking the initiative. If you initiate this plan and start to bring community organizations together, you'll most likely find others who have the same desire or have already started other initiatives.

Remember, this isn't an opportunity to profile your church. An initiative to combat suicide is about keeping teenagers in your community alive. Involve every church and organization in your community that has contact with teenagers and the families of teens.

Solicit the input, resources, and leadership from many organizations in the community. Your steering committee should represent a diverse population and multiple perspectives.

Consider bringing in an expert who can help consult with your team, inform parents, and coach community leaders and people who play a role in the lives of teens. Money is often available for such a consultant if organizations pool their resources. Don't be afraid to ask organizations for emergency funding.

Involve school district officials, police, fire, and rescue personnel, churches, park and recreation districts, youth centers or other organizations such as the YMCA, parent groups such as the PTA, student-parent organizations (including Mothers Against Drunk Driving, local crisis pregnancy centers, etc.), hospital and emergency medical teams, and concerned adolescent leaders.

Follow the plan closely. This isn't a time to initiate or showcase other agendas.

Resources on Teens and Depression and Suicide

| Section 4 |

4.1 AGENCIES

Start with your local hospital. If teens are depressed to the point of attempting suicide, they should seek emergency treatment at a hospital. From that point, long-term care can be administered, and the family can determine who will attend to that care and treatment.

If teens are desperate and seem ready to die, the best number to call is 911.

There are numerous suicide prevention hotlines. You may want to post these so teens know there is help available. All these lines are toll-free and staffed 24 hours a day, 7 days a week, by trained professionals. Calls are anonymous and confidential. These lines can give hurting teens immediate help. Some effective suicide hotlines are

- National Suicide Prevention Hotline: 1-800-SUICIDE (782-2433)
- National Hopeline Network: 1-800-273-TALK (8255)
- National Suicide Prevention (Deaf) Hotline: 1-800-799-4889

Suicide Prevention and Support Agencies

- Compassionate Friends: The mission of Compassionate Friends is to assist families toward positive resolution of grief following the death of a child of any age and provide information to help others be supportive. You can find support in your area from their Web site: http://www.compas sionatefriends.org

- The Jason Foundation Inc.: JFI produces educational materials that can help if you decide to do any suicide prevention training with teenagers. JFI's mission statement reads: "The Jason Foundation Inc. (JFI) is an educational organization dedicated to the awareness and prevention of youth suicide. JFI believes that awareness and education are the first steps to prevention. We want to establish a Triangle of Prevention by providing students, parents, and teachers/youth workers the tools and resources to possibly identify and help at-risk youth. This is accomplished through a series of programs and services that focus on information about the awareness and prevention of youth suicide." You can find their materials on their Web site: http://www.jasonfoundation.com

4.1B ONLINE RESOURCES

The Centers for Disease Control: The CDC has issued a plan of action, or template, to help prevent cluster suicides in a community. Church youth ministries should take the lead to know and initiate this plan in their communities. You can find the document entitled "CDC Recommendations for a Community Plan for the Prevention and Containment of Suicide Clusters" at http://www.cdc.gov/mmwr/preview/mmwrhtml/00001755.htm

American Foundation for Suicide Prevention: "The American Foundation for Suicide Prevention (AFSP) is the leading national not-for-profit organization exclusively dedicated to understanding and preventing suicide through research, education and advocacy, and to reaching out to people with mental disorders and those impacted by suicide."
http://www.afsp.org

Last Memories: (http://www.last-memories.com) This Web site provides free resources to create an online memorial page. It may be a great place to which you can direct teens who need to process their grief creatively.

4.1C BOOKS AND PRINTED MATERIALS

When Nothing Matters Anymore: A Survival Guide for Depressed Teens by Bev Cobain. This book is written to depressed teenagers by the cousin of the late Kurt Cobain. While not written from a Christian perspective, the book offers excellent insight and some helpful exercises for depressed teens to work through.

How I Stayed Alive When My Brain Was Trying to Kill Me: One Person's Guide to Suicide Prevention by Susan Blauner. This book is aimed at helping teens work through suicide ideation by walking them through a series of exercises geared at finding hope.

Adolescent Depression: A Guide for Parents by Francis Mark Mondimore, M.D. This book can help parents understand the physiological component of adolescent depression. Dr. Mondimore offers a thorough guide and explanation of the various antide-pressants used with teenagers and how those drugs work.

A Grief Observed by C. S. Lewis. This book may serve an older adolescent or youth worker well in working through grief. Lewis wrote this short book as a series of notes and journal entries after his wife died.

Turn My Mourning into Dancing by Henri Nouwen. This book offers a rich, contemplative, theological look at grief and death—great for youth workers and may serve a more mature teen well also.

notes

1. http://www.4therapy.com/consumer/life_topics/article/4252/110/When+Young +Kids+or+Teens+Suffer+With+Depression...

2. See http://www.pubmedcentral.nih.gov/articlerender.fcgi?artid=1414751#B3

3. See http://www.who.int/mental_health/media/en/62.pdf

4. See http://www.wma.net/e/policy/a9.htm

5. Centers For Disease Control, Web-based Injury Statistics Query and Reporting System (WISQRS); an interactive database system that provides customized reports of injury-related data. See http://www.cdc.gov/injury/wisqars/index. html

6. See http://webappa.cdc.gov/sasweb/ncipc/leadcaus.html

7. See http://www.surgeongeneral.gov/library/calltoaction/fact3.htm

8. See http://www.cdc.gov/ViolencePrevention/pdf/Suicide-DataSheet-a.pdf

9. Complicated grief is explored and explained more thoroughly in another book in this series, *What Do I Do When...Teenagers Deal with Death?*

10. For more about abuse, see *What Do I Do When...Teenagers Encounter Bullying and Violence?* in this series.

11. Tonja R. Nansel, Mary Overpeck, Ramani S. Pilla, W. June Ruan, Bruce Simons-Morton, and Peter Scheidt, "Bullying Behaviors Among US Youth: Prevalence and Association With Psychosocial Adjustment" Journal of the American Medical Association 285, no. 16 (2001): 2094-2100, http://jama-ama-assn.org/cgi/content/abstract/285/16/2094 (accessed 3/14/09).

12. For more information on adolescent bullying and violence, see the book in this series *What Do I Do When...Teenagers Encounter Bullying and Violence?*

13. See http://suicideandmentalhealthassociationinternational.org/suiconclust.html

14. See the book in this series entitled *What Do I Do When...Teenagers Deal with Death?* for more details on understanding how the death of a teenager affects parents and other family members.

In this series of books designed for anyone connected to teenagers, Dr. Steven Gerali addresses six daunting and difficult situations that, when they do happen, often leave youth workers and parents feeling unprepared. With a background in adolescent counseling, Dr. Gerali provides valuable resources to help youth workers and parents through some of the most challenging situations they may face.

Each book defines the issue, explores how different theological perspectives can impact the situation, offers helpful, practical tips, along with credible resources to help readers go deeper into the issues they're dealing with.

What Do I Do When Teenagers Encounter Bullying and Violence?
978-0-310-29194-7

What Do I Do When Teenagers Deal with Death?
978-0-310-29193-0

What Do I Do When Teenagers Are Victims of Abuse?
978-0-310-29195-4

What Do I Do When Teenagers Are Depressed and Contemplate Suicide?
978-0-310-29196-1

What Do I Do When Teenagers Struggle with Eating Disorders?
978-0-310-29197-8

What Do I Do When Teenagers Question Their Sexuality?
978-0-310-29198-5

Dr. Steven Gerali
Retail $6.99 each

Visit www.youthspecialties.com
or your local bookstore

youth
specialties

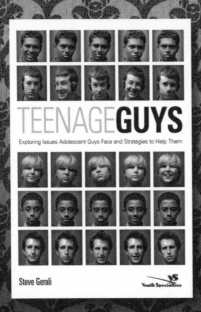

In *Teenage Guys*, author Steve Gerali breaks down the stages of development that adolescent guys go through, providing stories from his own experiences in ministry and counseling, as well as practical research findings to equip youth workers (both male and female) to more effectively minister to teenage guys. Each chapter includes advice from counselors and veteran youth workers, as well as discussion questions.

Teenage Guys
Exploring Issues Adolescent Guys Face and Strategies to Help Them

Steve Gerali
Retail $17.99
978-0-310-26985-4

Visit www.youthspecialties.com
or your local bookstore.